YOU HAVE ENOUGH FAITH

Stop Asking For More

By Ted Bowman

JC PUBLISHERS LLC

Winter Haven, Florida

Copyright © 2011 Ted Bowman

All rights reserved. This book or parts thereof may not be reproduced in any form, stored in a retrieval system or transmitted in any form by any means—electronic, mechanical, photocopying, recording or otherwise—without prior written permission of the publisher, except as provided by United States copyright law.

Unless otherwise noted, all Scripture quotations are from the King James Version of the Bible.

Scripture quotations marked NASB are from the New American Standard Bible. Copyright© 1960, 1962, 1963, 1968, 1971, 1972, 1973, 1975, 1977 by the Lockman Foundation. Used by permission.

Italics in Scriptures have been added by the author.

Cover photo by David Bowman.

Printed and bound in Canada by Art Bookbindery.
www.ArtBookbindery.com

ISBN 13: 978-0-9796899-1-8
ISBN 10: 0-9796899-1-0

I dedicate this book to my wife who has always been there for me when my own faith faltered over the years. Her constant reminder, "God's going to do what He said He would do," has kept me on course even in my darkest hours.

CONTENTS

Introduction		7
1	Faith Can Be a Confusing Subject	9
2	Faith Is Not About You and Me	27
3	Job Had an I Problem	39
4	Faith Makes You a Target	47
5	The Gates of Hell Are Stationary	57
6	Jesus, Always on Time	73
7	Waiting Is a Bummer	81
8	Don't Get Ahead of God	91
9	Cheer Up	101
10	Lord, Is That Really You?	107
11	Be Prepared for Mishaps	113
12	Storms Are Temporary	117
13	It's All About Who You Know	129
14	Won't They Come If We Have Miracles?	145
15	We Live for Him	151
Addendum		159
Bibliography		161
About the Author		163
Order Page		164

INTRODUCTION

Ask a Christian to define faith and he will robotically quote Hebrews 11:1: "Now faith is the substance of things hoped for, the evidence of things not seen." Ask several Christians to define the verse and you will hear a variety of answers. We are as guilty today as the Pharisees of Jesus' time. Give us a chance and we will complicate the simple gospel of Christ beyond all recognition.

Years ago, I read a four-page article on faith in a major Christian magazine. After reading the extensive article, I was no closer to understanding faith. Recently, I discussed the subject of faith with a fellow minister. After his rather lengthy explanation of faith, I said, "That's confusing to me."

"Well, what's your definition of faith?" he asked with a hint of disapproval.

Quoting Arndt and Gingrich's classic definition, I said, "Trust in and reliance on God."

My friend looked at me as if I just offered him a glass of sour milk. Perhaps my definition was too simple.

My definition of faith has evolved over the years in favor of simplicity. As I studied faith, the word *obedience* kept jumping out at me. The old song "Trust and Obey" says it best. I have never been disappointed or hurt by trusting and obeying God and neither will you.

Chapter 1

FAITH CAN BE A CONFUSING SUBJECT

But the ship was . . . tossed with waves (Matthew 14:24)

I have struggled with faith since accepting Christ as a seventeen-year-old. I remember a Christian friend in our youth group saying, "Faith means you just pretend it's going to happen and it happens." Hard as I tried, that never seemed to work for me. At the same time, that pretend exercise seems to emphasize simple expectation. After all, "Faith is the substance [reality] of things hoped for, the evidence [proof] of things not seen" (Heb. 11:1). The words "reality" and "proof" are the suggested literal translations of the words "substance" and "evidence," according to Alfred Marshall's Interlinear Greek-English New Testament. Simply put, faith is expecting what you hope for.

Hebrews 11:1 is the Christian's favored response to the question, "What is faith?" Ask ten believers to explain what Hebrews 11:1 means, however, and answers will vary. Believers in other countries, especially in poorer areas of the world, seem to have more faith than we do in America. Extraordinary miracles occur on a regular basis. A friend recently suggested something that got my attention. He said,

"Christians in other countries don't have any more faith than we do—they just don't have any doubt."

Evidently, when it comes to faith, they just expect things to happen and they do.

THE BOY WHO HAS NO EYES

My friend Arthur Leis was a missionary in Africa for a third of a century. He visited me in South Carolina and shared a miracle he witnessed in Uganda. As he preached through a translator in a local church one evening, he quoted the verse, "For with God, nothing shall be impossible" (Luke 1:37). The audience reacted and the men began to talk to each other. Noticing the positive response, Arthur kept repeating the verse and, as he did, the congregation grew more and more talkative. Finally, the men stood and began to walk out. Confused, Arthur asked what was happening.

The pastor explained, "Since you told them, 'With God, nothing is impossible,' they have decided this must be the night God will heal the boy who has no eyes."

Assuming the boy was blind, Arthur quickly admitted he had no faith for something like that and said he'd rather not go. The pastor cautioned him, saying, "If we don't go, they will be insulted."

Reluctantly, Arthur followed the pastor and his people. They made their way to a hut in the village and went inside. What Arthur saw shocked him. The boy wasn't just blind—he had no eyeballs. His eyelids were shut and sunken, revealing empty sockets. As the pastor began a simple prayer, a bright light flooded the dimly lit room. Arthur said he watched in amazement as the boy's eyelids slowly bulged outward. Moments later, the eyelids cracked open to reveal what looked like two hard-boiled eggs.

The pastor, standing by the boy, said, "Lord, he has no brown spots in his eyes. If you don't give him the brown spots, he won't be able to see."

Seconds later, a tiny dot appeared on each eyeball. The dots slowly morphed into brown irises. Pupils quickly formed, and the boy began to see for the first time in his life.

That child is now a young man preaching in the many churches God started through a humble missionary named Arthur Leis. If you ask him about his part in the event, Arthur will insist he only witnessed the miracle and admonish you to give God all the credit. He said the experience changed him forever. Those precious people had no doubt.

LORD, INCREASE OUR FAITH

We spend a lot of time trying to understand why miracles are rare today. We tend to blame ourselves and say we don't have enough faith. I found only one place in the New Testament where anyone ever asked for more faith. "And the apostles said unto the Lord, Increase our faith" (Luke 17:5). Marshall's literal translation reads, "Add to us faith" instead of, "Increase our faith."

The idea of *more* faith isn't really the focus. They simply asked for faith. In response, Jesus said, "If you had faith like a mustard seed, you would say to this mulberry tree, 'Be uprooted and planted in the sea;' and it would obey you" (Luke 17:6 NASB). Jesus seemed to suggest even minute faith can produce miraculous results. It's not the amount of faith, but the mere existence of faith that spurs God to move supernaturally.

Matthew records another mustard seed illustration when the disciples failed to cast a demon from a child. "Why could not we cast him out?" they asked.

And Jesus said unto them, *"Because of your unbelief:* for verily I say unto you, If ye have faith as a grain of mustard seed, ye shall say unto this mountain, Remove hence to yonder place; and it shall remove; and nothing shall be impossible to you" (Mt. 17:20, emphasis mine). The word "unbelief" literally means "little faith," but the root meaning is "faithlessness, untrustiness; distrust, unbelief," according to Bullinger. When you hear Christ use the term "little faith," the root meaning is *faithlessness* or *no faith at all*.

FAITH IS TRUSTING, NOT TRYING

I am aware the Bible says, "faith without works is dead" (James 2:20). James is simply saying faith will naturally lead to works. Simply put, action is a natural offshoot of faith. Yet, works will never produce faith. As usual, we tend to reverse the order. Faith is trusting, not trying, but when you fully trust God, you will act accordingly. To paraphrase James 2:15-16, "If a brother or sister needs clothing and food, you don't just tell them it will be all right—you give them clothes and food." Faith without works is just words.

Some believe fasting is a prerequisite to casting out demons. Be assured, I believe fasting is important to believers in every age. My point is this: if fasting is required to cast out demons then something beyond faith is necessary. Scripture teaches otherwise.

"And having summoned His twelve disciples, He gave them authority over unclean spirits, to cast them out, and to heal every kind of disease and every kind of sickness" (Mt. 10:1 NASB). According to Luke, Jesus shortly thereafter expanded His efforts and sent out seventy disciples in pairs with the same empowerment. There is no indication the disciples fasted. They just went, no doubt filled with hopeful expectation.

Luke adds, "And the seventy returned with joy, saying, 'Lord, even the demons are subject to us in Your name'"

(Luke 10:17 NASB). The disciples were surprised they could cast out devils with such ease.

Jesus responded to their joy, saying, "Behold, I have given you authority to tread on serpents and scorpions, and over all the power of the enemy, and nothing shall injure you. Nevertheless, do not rejoice in this, that the spirits are subject to you, but rejoice that your names are recorded in heaven" (Luke 10:19-20 NASB). Your salvation and relationship with God are more important than your ministry.

Why do we tend to make casting out demons contingent on fasting instead of just following the instruction of Christ? Suppose you unexpectedly face a situation that requires exercising faith immediately and you haven't fasted lately. I know I said faith is trusting, not trying, but at a given point in our spiritual growth, acting on our faith becomes natural. Trying becomes irresistible. We just start doing what He says. Fasting has its place, but should not be seen as some sort of payment to gain power with God.

A friend fought a bout with sickness for several days. A well-meaning Christian called to say she was praying. My sick friend said, "Right now I don't need prayer—I need someone to clean my house." Unlike the prayerful but inactive friend, the immature, undisciplined disciples just went and did what Jesus told them. They didn't spend days fasting, praying, and preparing their hearts. They just acted on Christ's command.

As I said, I believe in fasting and prayer. Both efforts will help focus our minds for ministry and are a necessary part of our devotion. I just don't believe they are a prerequisite to casting out devils or healing the sick. Why would Christ require of us what He never required of the disciples? Consider further, this was before any disciples experienced the infilling of the Holy Spirit at Pentecost. They fasted and prayed then—not because they needed extra power to cast out demons or work miracles, but out of sheer love and devotion. They fasted to clear their minds and hearts from earth's distractions.

As a young evangelist, I spent much time in prayer before each service. I subconsciously believed the more I prayed, the better chance I had that God would anoint me for powerful ministry. One day, I spent extra time in prayer, hopeful I would experience a mightier move of God as I preached. The service was good but not exceptional. The next day, the pastor insisted I go fishing with him. I had little time to pray. That night, the Holy Spirit moved in an extraordinary way. I was dumfounded. In time I realized the Lord wanted me to trust Him and not my preparation. By all means, fast and pray, but realize at the outset—this is God's ministry, not ours. It's never about what we do. It's always about what He does. It's not what I will do for Him that matters—it's what He will do through me.

The disciples of John addressed the question of fasting when they asked Jesus, "Why do we and the Pharisees fast oft, but thy disciples fast not?"

"And Jesus said unto them, Can the children of the bridechamber mourn as long as the bridegroom is with them? but the days will come when the bridegroom shall be taken from them, and then shall they fast" (Mt. 9:14–15). We fast today, not to procure power, but out of devotion to Him who said, "Follow Me."

Fasting brings focus. Unger's Bible Dictionary expresses the Biblical meaning of fasting: "After the Jewish custom, fasting was frequently joined with prayer that the mind, unencumbered with earthly matter, might devote itself with less distraction to the contemplation of divine things." Fasting helps rid us of the mental clutter that comes from modern, fast-paced living. I fast, not to gain power with God, but to re-focus my mind on His purpose and will. Fasting minimizes what I want and maximizes what He wants.

WE TEND TO REVERSE THE DIVINE ORDER

While writing this chapter, I called my dear friend and former college professor, Dr. Duran Palmertree, to ask him a few questions about faith. As usual, he was a fountain of useful information. He suggested most of us believe it takes a mountain of faith to move a mustard seed. I laughed and agreed. We do tend to reverse the divine order of things. For example, as a teenager, I interpreted Galatians 5:16 in reverse. It says, "Walk in the Spirit, and ye shall not fulfil the lust of the flesh."

I immediately set about the task of not fulfilling the lust of the flesh, so I could walk in the Spirit.

Paul loved to say the same thing two different ways to make a point. He talked about walking in the Spirit two verses earlier. "For all the law is fulfilled in one word, even in this; Thou shalt love thy neighbor as thyself. But if ye bite and devour one another, take heed that ye be not consumed one of another. This I say then, [To put it another way] Walk in the Spirit, and ye shall not fulfil the lust of the flesh" (Gal. 5:14-16). How do we walk in the Spirit? According to Paul, we walk in the Spirit by loving our neighbor as ourselves.

In other words, learning to love Scripturally is the first step to spiritual growth. Learning to love God's way is not our goal—it is the foundation of all the rest.

MINISTRY AND SPEAR-THROWING DON'T MESH WELL

Evidently you can be spiritual without love. King Saul prophesied one day and tried to spear David the next. Ministry and spear throwing don't mesh well. Paul adds this footnote: "If I speak with the tongues of men and of angels, but do not have love, I am become a noisy gong or a clanging cymbal. And if I have the gift of prophecy and know all mysteries and all knowledge; and if I have all faith, so as to remove mountains, but do not have love, I am nothing" (1 Cor. 13:1-2 NASB). Without love as our foundation, we have no basis for growth. Love paves the road to maturity. Love is the key to faith. Learning to love God's way makes radical faith possible.

God's love liberates us from selfish motives that can choke faith. His selfless love sets us free to trust Him in every situation. Mature love compels us to love even those who would crucify us. Do you really want to be like Jesus? Let Him teach you how to love the fervent but misguided believers who carry hammers and nails.

Jesus, in Mark, talks about what we often refer to as "mustard seed" faith when He says, "Have faith in God. Truly I say to you, whoever says to this mountain, 'Be taken up and cast into the sea,' and does not doubt in his heart, but believes that what he says is going to happen, it shall be granted him. Therefore I say to you, all things for which you pray and ask, believe that you have received them, and they shall be granted you" (Mark 11:22-24 NASB).

There you have it. Trust in and rely on God without doubting and walk in expectant hope. As I said, believers in other countries experience the miraculous more often than we do here in America. Is it possible they don't have more faith—they just don't have any doubt? Could it be they just *do* instead of preparing to do? Traditional wisdom insists faith is trusting, not trying. Nevertheless, at a given point, trusting God may no longer be enough. Consistent and persistent trusting should eventually make acting on your faith an irresistible urge. Instead of making great plans to do exploits for God, why don't we just start doing all things through Christ?

GOD IS A FATHER WHO JUST HAPPENS TO BE GOD

We should always remember the unchanging fact that God is, and always has been a Father because He has always had a Son. As an earthly father with limited resources, I will do everything humanly possible to provide for my children. Our heavenly Father will do anything in His unlimited power to take care of His family. God is called Father six times in the Old Testament. The New Testament calls Him Father some three hundred times. He is trying to tell us something. God wants a family. It seems His favorite role is being a Father. As my friend, Pastor Bob Simmons, says, *God is a Father who just happens to be God.* Paul agrees and says, "And because ye are sons, God hath sent forth the Spirit of His Son into your hearts, crying, Abba, Father" (Gal. 4:6). According to Unger's Bible Dictionary, *Ábba* "was in common use in the mixed Aramaic dialect of Palestine, and was used by children in addressing their father. It answers to our word, *papa*."

A good earthly father is easy to trust. Our heavenly Father is utterly trustworthy. We can always trust in and rely on our Father with complete confidence. Picture a typical two-year-old playing, laughing, and rolling on the floor. He has no concern about his next meal, clean clothes, or anything else he might need. He rightfully expects food, clothing, and tender care. God is our Creator and, yes, our eventual judge. Nevertheless, He forever remains an all-sufficient, all-caring Father bent on supplying His children's every need. Before the first act of creation, God had a Son. He was a Father before time began. He is, now and forever, our loving heavenly Father, our *Papa*. Because He is our Father, we can know without question, if He commands us to do something, He will empower us to do it. He is Jehovah-Jireh: "Jehovah will see (to it)" (Strong). We can safely assume, God will provide *what He demands*. He will see to it that we have the capability to do what He tells us.

Paul admonishes us to "think soberly, according as God has dealt to every man the measure of faith" (Rom. 12:3). The Greek word for "measure" is "metron," and means "a limited *portion (degree):*—measure" (Strong). Allow me to paraphrase. *God has given you a measure [specified amount] of faith and that will prove to be enough. You won't need more.* Satan's biggest lie has always been, "You need more; you don't have enough." He tempted Eve by suggesting she needed more knowledge.

"For God doth know that in the day ye eat thereof [the tree of the knowledge of good and evil], then your eyes shall be opened, and ye shall be as [like] gods, knowing good and evil" (Gen. 3:5). Did you catch Satan's second subtle lie? Adam and Eve were already like God—"And God said, Let us make man in our image, after our likeness" (Gen. 1:26).

Satan wants you to focus on your alleged needs. God wants you to focus on His Son and His full provision. The Father's first recorded words in the New Testament could be its underlying theme. It reads, "This is my beloved son: hear him" (Luke 9:35). True faith centers on Christ and looks nowhere else. Looking at ourselves will always produce frustration and a sense of lack. Looking at Christ makes us aware of His full provision and prompts us to declare, "I can do all things through Him who strengthens me" (Phil. 4:13 NASB).

As a young Christian, I constantly felt I needed more of God. At least, that was what preachers and teachers seemed to suggest. Over time, I began to realize I didn't need more of God—I had all of God in Christ. "For in Him [Christ] dwelleth all the fulness of the Godhead bodily. And ye are complete in [having been filled with] Him" (Col. 2:9-10). Paul's prayer for the Ephesian Christians ended with the words, "know the love of Christ, which passeth knowledge, that ye might be filled with all the fulness of God" (Eph. 3:19). When we know the love of Christ, the fullness of God resides in us.

Two thousand years ago God gave us everything He had in Christ, and promptly went out of the giving business. "According as His divine power hath given unto us all things that pertain unto life and godliness" (2 Pet. 1:3, emphasis mine). He didn't give us some things or certain things—He gave us *all* things. I'm fully aware He still gives us our daily bread and supplies all our temporal needs. Those are ongoing material necessities. In the Spirit realm, Christ has already provided resources to meet every spiritual need.

Stop asking for what you already have. It's an insult to Christ's sacrifice and Calvary's full provision.

WE LACK NOTHING IF WE HAVE CHRIST

God no longer gives us things—He gives us Christ. Do you want love? "God is love" (1 John 4:8). Do you need peace? "For He is our peace" (Eph. 2:14). Do you want power? "Christ [is] the power of God" (1 Cor. 1:24). Do you desire wisdom, righteousness, sanctification, or redemption? "But of him are ye in Christ Jesus, who of God is made unto us wisdom, and righteousness, and sanctification, and redemption" (1 Cor. 1:30).

Paul tells us where to find all wisdom and knowledge. "In whom [Christ] are hid all the treasures of wisdom and knowledge" (Col. 2:3). Christ in us means we have access to all wisdom and knowledge. Lest we get full of ourselves, the Holy Spirit reminds us, "But we have this treasure in earthen vessels, that the excellency of the power may be of God and not of us" (2 Cor. 4:7).

It is hard to fathom why God would put the priceless treasure of His Son in common clay pots like you and me. Perhaps He wanted to make it difficult for us to fall into pride. Christ is the source of all wisdom and knowledge. He is the true treasure. He is our free and unlimited access to all wisdom and knowledge. Such beautiful treasure in common clay pots speaks of His unselfish love.

Where does the Holy Spirit fit in all this? Christ tells us: "Howbeit, when he, the Spirit of truth, is come, he will guide you into all truth: for he shall not speak of himself; but whatsoever he shall hear, that shall he speak: and he will shew you things to come" (John 16:13). What does the Holy Spirit hear? Conversations between the Father and the Son about you and me. Christ continues: "He shall glorify me, for he shall receive of mine, and shall shew it unto you. All things that the Father hath are mine: therefore said I, that he shall take of mine, and shall shew it unto you" (John 16:14-15).

Rely on the promises of God in His word, but always focus on Christ. If you must look within, look at Christ ten times before you look at yourself even once. Looking within, incidentally, only results in one of two undesirable things. You are either conscious of failure, which brings guilt and depression, or you are doing well, which often leads to pride. Depression leads to misery and neither pride nor misery are part of the fruit of the Spirit.

It's not about you and me—it's about Him. The less we focus on ourselves, the more we will experience Him. We have been crucified with Christ and we no longer live. Yet, because He lives, we live also. Because He does, we can do. Just remember: "Whatever you do, do all to the glory of God" (1 Cor. 10:31 NASB). It really is about Him and His glory. The fact that He includes us in all this is still hard to grasp.

As a young evangelist, I developed a message on hungering and thirsting for God. I based it on David's prayer: "As the hart panteth after the water brooks, so panteth my soul after thee, O God. My soul thirsteth for God, for the living God: when shall I come and appear before God?" (Ps. 42:1-2).

I found several verses to support my sermon. We preachers love our concordances. Typically we will pray until we get a thought. We assume it must be from God, but to be safe, we muse, *I wonder if there is any Scripture to back that up.* Out comes the concordance.

THEN SOMETHING HAPPENED THAT CHANGED EVERYTHING

For years, I preached my message on the Christian's need to hunger and thirst for God. Then something happened that changed everything. The Lord challenged me one day to stop reading the Bible to verify what I already believed and dare to read His Word just to see what it said. It didn't affect any of my basic doctrinal positions, but it did wreak havoc on some of my favorite sermons, including my message on hungering and thirsting for God. Everything was fine as long as I skipped over verses that didn't fit my theory. Reality set in quickly when I stopped ignoring bothersome verses that went against the point I wanted to make.

The Bible is its own best commentary. Jesus has the last word on our alleged need to be hungry and thirsty for God. He said, "I am the bread of life: he that cometh to me shall *never* hunger; and he that believeth on me shall *never* thirst" (John 6:35, emphasis mine). Hunger for Him when in need of forgiveness, but rest in His provision from then on and enjoy His guaranteed fullness.

Jesus told the Samaritan woman as she offered Him a drink of water, "Whosoever drinketh of this water shall thirst again: But whosoever drinketh of the water that I shall give him shall *never* thirst; but the water that I shall give him shall be in him a well of water springing up into everlasting life" (John 4:13-14, emphasis mine).

I remember the old admonition, "Get under the spout where the glory comes out." It seemed plausible at the time. I spent lots of time and energy as a young Christian trying to get under that spout. Realizing I had a well inside set me free.

THERE MAY BE SOME LEAKAGE

I remember teaching that suggested we can be filled with glory on Sunday, but there may be some leakage during the week. We are encouraged to attend the mid-week service to replenish our supply. Certainly, between Wednesday and Sunday, more leakage may occur, so Sunday attendance is strongly advised. I can hear the faithful now: "Everybody grab your buckets; it's time for church." Can you imagine the sound of the pails clanging against the doors as they get in and out of their cars? Everyone is hopeful as the service begins. When a preacher says, "If you are here to get a blessing, say amen," we automatically focus on our own needs instead of the needs of others.

I don't mean to be unkind, but isn't that the way we think at times? To be clear, I fully recognize the need for spiritual renewal. We believers need those renewing experiences "when the times of refreshing shall come from the presence of the Lord" (Acts 3:19). I am also aware we can be re-filled with the Spirit from time to time. In Acts 2:4, the remnant of Christ's followers was filled with the Holy Spirit on the Day of Pentecost. Two chapters later, we read, "And when they had prayed, the place was shaken where they were assembled together; and they were all filled with the Holy Ghost, and they spoke the word of God with boldness" (Acts 4:31). As the old Pentecostal preachers put it, *One filling—many re-fillings.*

My question is, "What is the source of your spiritual water supply?"

THROW YOUR BUCKET AWAY

The water of life flows from Christ and it's free. "And the Spirit and the bride say, Come. And let him that heareth say, Come. And let him that is athirst come. And whosoever will, let him take the water of life freely" (Rev. 22:17). When you realize the truth about Jesus and the water He provides, He becomes your water supply. You become the well. Throw your bucket away. You can stop living with hunger and thirst and start feeding others and quenching their thirst. Throw your bucket away and become a giver instead of a taker. Throw your bucket away and become a funnel of refreshing that comes from the presence of the Lord.

Exercising your faith from a perspective of fullness is much easier than struggling to believe in a parched desert. It's the difference between night and day, cold and hot, and doubt and mountain-moving faith. Throw your bucket away—you have a well inside. His name is Jesus.

Faith needs a positive foundation and a proper mindset to work effectively. You don't need more faith—you need a fresh perspective. Focus on Him, rest in Him, and accept His full provision. You have a lot to give away. After telling His disciples to "heal the sick, cleanse the lepers, raise the dead, cast out devils," Jesus added, "Freely have you received; freely give" (Mt. 10:8).

Stop asking for more faith and get busy giving. Jesus said, "If any man is thirsty, let him come to Me and drink. He who believes in Me, as the Scripture said, 'From his innermost being shall flow rivers of living water'" (John 7:37–38 NASB). Stop trying to soak up blessings and start spilling over. Think Niagara Falls.

STOP LIVING IN ADAM'S POVERTY

There is a major difference between asking God to supply all your needs and recognizing your God-given right to walk in the fullness of Christ with all your needs fully met. When can you start walking in fullness? Right now! Stop living in Adam's poverty and start walking in Christ's fullness. Stop thinking about your lack and start thanking God for His guaranteed fullness.

Christianity is not about what we need. Christianity is about what we already have in Christ. "And of His fullness have all we received, and grace for grace" (John 1:16). Christ died and rose again so we could enjoy God in all His glory right here on Earth. Because of Calvary, we are children of God with all the rights of sonship. "But as many as received him, to them gave he power [right and authority] to become the sons [children] of God, even to them that believe on his name" (John 1:12).

You can start enjoying God's fullness today and be continually satisfied. As Jesus Himself explains, "Blessed are they which do hunger and thirst after righteousness: for they shall be filled" (Mt. 5:6). Marshall translates saying, "for they shall be satisfied." I know it sounds too easy, but dare to believe it.

It may take some mental effort to enlarge your thinking. Focus on Christ and His fullness. Drop the popular "What about me?" mindset. If you must look inside yourself, see only the Christ of glory. Focus on Christ and His blessings will gravitate toward you. Moses told the children of Israel, "And all these blessings shall come on thee, and overtake thee, if thou shalt hearken unto the voice of the Lord thy God" (Deut. 28:2). I'm thinking about writing a book titled *SPIRITUAL WHIPLASH: Rear-ended by the Blessings of God.*

I'M ABOUT TO BE HAPPY

Years ago, I preached a revival in a small local church. After a week of services, a man stood and said, "I didn't know what to think about some of the things this young preacher was saying, but for the first time in twenty years, I'm about to be happy." Maybe he started focusing more on Christ than himself.

Many believers walk where you walk. I did for years. It's an easy habit to form—just follow the crowd. The truths we embrace depend on our point of view. Applied to church life, that means you will adopt the mindset of the church family you joined as a new Christian. We all tend to see through denominational glasses. We usually accept what we learn from spiritual leaders we trust and tend to believe it without question. Yet no one has a monopoly on the truth. At the same time, we all have access to God's word.

When the Bereans heard Paul and Silas preach, they "received the word with all readiness of mind, and searched the scriptures daily, whether those things were so" (Acts 17:11). They didn't just accept what they heard—they verified it in Scripture. Perhaps we should develop the same habit. Wouldn't it be interesting if you interrupted your pastor one Sunday morning and said, "Excuse me, pastor, do you have any Scripture to back up what you just said?"

I preached a meeting in Florida years ago and invited listeners to do just that. The series of services concluded on Easter Sunday. In the middle of the Easter morning message, a hand went up on the back row.

"Brother Ted, I've got a question."

I responded, "Yes, Joe, what is it?"

Visitors looked around in disbelief. I answered his question and continued as if nothing happened. I welcomed the interruption.

How many times have you heard a preacher say something that puzzled you? Wouldn't it be nice to get an explanation right then? I don't know if the church is ready for that. Meanwhile, if you can find a way to remove your doctrinal glasses and read the Bible just to see what it says, you may find a freshness that is truly liberating. Start adjusting your faith-focus from yourself to Him and your confusion will begin to evaporate.

After all, "God is not the author of confusion, but of peace" (1 Cor. 14:33). Focus on the author of peace.

Chapter 2

FAITH IS NOT ABOUT YOU AND ME

Jesus went unto them (Matthew 14:25)

Psychiatrists tell us we think about ourselves ninety-five percent of the time. We are basically selfish. As a result, the blood of Christ is not enough—we need the cross. The blood solves the problem of our sins; the cross addresses the problem of self. We accept Christ's blood sacrifice for our sins and mistakenly overlook our need for the work of the cross. The point I'm trying to make is simple: Faith withers when we spend too much time thinking about ourselves. When self is dominant, faith can be elusive.

You will never learn to walk by faith while you focus on yourself. If we interpret Calvary in terms of how it will benefit us, we are still ruled by the spirit of this world. We tend to look within ourselves most of the time. Much less often, we look to the Lord. If we could train ourselves to look at Him more than we look at ourselves, only God knows what might happen.

Hebrews 12:2 is helpful. It says, "Looking unto Jesus the author and finisher of our faith; who for the joy that was set before him endured the cross, despising the shame, and is set down at the right hand of the throne of God." Marshall's interlinear translation begins verse 2 with the words, "Looking away from, unto Jesus."

HUMAN EYES CAN ONLY FOCUS IN ONE DIRECTION

Many birds can look in two directions at once. I had a parakeet that would look me in the face with one eye and watch my hand with his other eye as I stroked his tail. God made us differently. Human eyes can only focus in one direction. Paraphrased, Hebrews 12:2 reads, "Looking [away from all that distracts] unto Jesus, the source and completer of our faith." You don't need more faith. You just need to refocus your faith on a new target—Christ.

Some of the old church hymns are beautiful and full of truth. Perhaps you remember the words, "Turn your eyes upon Jesus. Look full in His wonderful face, and the things of earth will grow strangely dim in the light of His glory and grace." As you focus on Christ, self will start to fade from sight as well. Don't get rid of your mirrors—just see Christ in the background as you as get ready to face the day.

I want to address an issue that has concerned me for years. It has to do with what we refer to as *The Word*. Of course, I'm talking about the Bible. No matter how I approach this, some may be uncomfortable with a few things I'm about to say. Hear me out, please.

I believe in reading the Bible daily. Every believer should read the Bible as much as possible, but there is a common belief about Bible reading that concerns me. Recently, I heard a prominent pastor on television say, "If you don't know the Word, you can't know the Lord."

It sounded reasonable at the time. Preachers admonish us with common clichés like *Read* the Word, *internalize* the Word, *work* the Word, *stay* in the Word, *know* the Word and *live* the Word, just to name a few.

Here is my point. Reading the Bible is wonderful and spiritually beneficial—*if* you can read.

"Nearly half of America's adults are poor readers or 'functionally illiterate.' They can't carry out simple tasks like balancing check books, reading drug labels, or writing essays for a job" (National Adult Literacy Survey of 1993).

"44 million adults in the U.S. can't read well enough to read a simple story to a child" (National Adult Literacy Survey, 1992, NCED, U.S. Department of Education).

"21 million Americans can't read at all, 45 million are marginally illiterate and one-fifth of high school graduates can't read their diplomas" (Department of Justice, 1993).

Current statistics reflect only a small improvement in those numbers.

Most are ashamed to admit their illiteracy, so those who attend church must feel doubly guilty every time the preacher chides the congregation for not reading the Bible enough. Are we suggesting these folks can't know the Lord? Believers in countries around the world enjoy intimate relationships with God and see miracles on a regular basis. Many of them can't read their own language.

I have a Christian friend who works in construction. Our families attended the same church for a number of years. He is skilled at his craft, but he can't read. He signs his name with an X. I have signed as his witness on legal documents. He is a wonderful Christian, deeply in love with Jesus. His spirit is beautiful, and he definitely knows and enjoys the Lord. I admire his faith.

When I was a Christian school principal I had a sixth-grade student who told me her dad couldn't read. He was a mortgage broker. She read his contracts to him so he felt safe signing off on them. These folks are sitting on the pews in your local church.

HE NEVER READ THE BIBLE

Traditional teaching refers to Abraham as "the father of faith," yet he never read the Bible. James used him as an example of a man with true faith. "Abraham believed God, and it was imputed [reckoned] unto him for righteousness: and he was called the Friend of God" (James 2:23). Marshall's Interlinear inserts the term "reckoned" because that is the literal meaning. According to Bullinger, "reckon" is an accounting term and means, "to occupy one's self with reckonings or calculations." Our faith becomes our righteousness in the bank of God. Count on it.

Abraham knew God more intimately than anyone alive today would dare claim, yet he never read a verse of Scripture. The Bible didn't exist and the Ten Commandments wouldn't arrive for four centuries. Is it possible to know God intimately without knowing the Word? Abraham proved it was completely possible.

God knew Abraham so intimately, He wouldn't destroy Sodom until He checked with Abraham to ask his opinion. In Genesis 18:17 we read, "And the Lord said, Shall I hide from Abraham that thing which I do?" God then had the famous bartering session with Abraham. "And Abraham drew near, and said, Wilt thou also destroy the righteous with the wicked?" (Gen. 18:23). The bargaining began with Abraham saying, "Peradventure there be fifty righteous within the city: wilt thou also destroy and not spare the place for the fifty righteous that are therein?" (v. 24).

God quickly agreed to spare Sodom for the sake of fifty righteous people. Abraham continued to barter in descending increments and each time God agreed to spare the city. "Would you spare the city for forty-five? forty? thirty? twenty?" After Abraham induced God to agree not to destroy the city for "ten's sake" (v. 32), something interesting happened. God left. "And the Lord went his way" (v. 33).

He knew where Abraham was going with his argument. Between Lot, his wife, and his two virgin daughters, there were at least four righteous people in Sodom. If you throw in one or two family friends of like faith, the number of righteous could reach five or six. Chances are Abraham's next number would be five and God would have been obliged to spare Sodom. That wasn't an option.

At a given point, the God of love must act as a righteous judge, but only after His mercy has been stretched paper-thin, and long after men have hardened their hearts in permanent rebellion against a loving God. Abraham knew God intimately enough to barter with lives in the balance. How did Abraham get to know God without the aid of Scripture? Can we? I'm sure of it. Read the Bible faithfully if you can. If you don't read very well, stop feeling guilty and start enjoying your God.

I MADE IT MY PERSONAL GOAL TO STRAIGHTEN OUT THE ENTIRE BODY OF CHRIST

Too often, preachers talk more about behavior than character. Christ wants to build our character. I believe focusing on behavior is the result of a man-centered approach to ministry. Faith cannot flourish in a self-centered atmosphere. I used to be a hard, judgmental preacher. I focused on behavior. As a result, I didn't really enjoy my Christian experience. When I graduated from Bible college, I entered ministry as a young evangelist. Convinced I knew what was wrong with the church, I proceeded to declare it everywhere. I made it my personal goal to straighten out the entire body of Christ, one church at a time. I knew about His judgment and that was about it.

My attitude was terrible. All I could see were problems that needed correcting. My focus was entirely man-centered. If Jesus had my attitude, He would have walked up to blind Bartimaeus, shook a finger in his face, and shouted, "You're blind!" Then He would have walked away saying, "I sure told him the truth."

That might have been the truth, but Bartimaeus would still be in the dark.

WE'RE ALREADY FAMILIAR WITH OUR PERSONAL FAILURES

The real problem is simple. We're already familiar with our personal failures. Satan reminds us every day of our faults. The last thing we believers need is some preacher constantly reminding us of our shortcomings. A minister who sends you home feeling condemned and guilty needs to find other employment. The Gospel of Jesus Christ is *good* news. "There is therefore now no condemnation [guilty verdict] for those who are in Christ Jesus" (Rom. 8:1 NASB). I know we need correction and even rebuke occasionally, but not almost every time we go to church. We're already Satan's target—we don't need to be in the preacher's crosshairs.

Every church service should remind us that we are loved, and there is hope. The world is negative; the print media is negative; network news is negative; the medical community is negative and, it seems, most politicians are negative.

Young preachers, I beg you—find a way to be positive and uplifting. God's people need encouragement in a world that grows more negative by the day. Let the Holy Spirit do the correcting. If a believer's heart is open, he will accept God's judgment. If his heart is closed, neither you nor God can change his mind. God won't violate man's free will and neither should we.

Would you like to feel better about life in general? Leave the television off for a few days. The news is especially negative. It's not just the gory stories that lead, but the dialogue that usually ends on a negative note right down to the weather report. Example: "There is only a ten percent chance of rain today, but you might take your umbrella, just to be safe."

The Apostle Paul would have made a terrible reporter. A news anchor would quote Romans 6:23 like this: "The gift of God is eternal life through Jesus Christ our Lord, *but the wages of sin is death*" (emphasis mine). The Holy Spirit inspired Paul to pen, "For the wages of sin is death; but the gift of God is eternal life through Jesus Christ our Lord" (Rom. 6:23). The Gospel of Christ focuses on life, not death; joy, not sadness; light, not darkness; and faith, not doubt.

In my early ministry, I preached Wednesday through two Sundays in a typical, ten-day evangelistic crusade. We called them *revivals*. The Holy Spirit had time to do wonderful things because we didn't feel constrained to rush. The first Sunday night of a revival in a church in northern Indiana, still focusing on the negative, I railed against the people, accusing them of not praying enough, and not really wanting revival. What a tragedy! I didn't know their hearts. Frankly, looking back, I didn't know much of anything.

The next evening, the pastor met me on the front steps of the church and said we needed to talk. I had been in full-time ministry for about a year. But for that conversation, I would have left the ministry early as a disillusioned, bitter young man. I wasn't enjoying preaching and I didn't know why.

The pastor started apologetically saying, "I may lose you as a friend, Ted, but I have to share some things with you." He went on to explain the shambles the church had been in only eighteen months earlier when he took over as pastor. Attendance was below fifty. The people were discouraged and ready to give up. For over a year, the pastor knocked on doors all over the neighborhood. He found a number of former church families who drifted away when the church began to have problems and he successfully persuaded many of them to come back. Church attendance grew to one hundred-fifty. The first Sunday night of the meeting, the pastor said he counted one hundred-sixty people. He admitted the church still wasn't where he wanted it to be spiritually, but it was growing and the people were excited.

Here is the sad part of the story. That first Sunday night, the members brought dozens of unchurched folk who really needed the Lord. The pastor said, "Ted, if you had preached any kind of evangelistic message last night and given a simple altar invitation, you would have seen two or three dozen people come forward and give their lives to Christ. Instead, you chastised my people for not praying enough or caring enough. You didn't even give an altar call."

Stunned and humiliated, I dug into my store of sermon outlines and found the most uplifting message possible. I preached with nothing inside me. The people responded with rejoicing and enthusiasm. I could hardly believe it. I have tried to preach positive, uplifting messages from that day to this. I thanked that wise pastor several times over the years for daring to confront me in love.

I WAS GUILTY OF A COMMON MISCONCEPTION

We're still talking about faith. A positive attitude will prompt you to be encouraging and uplifting. I was guilty of a common misconception. I zeroed in on behavior—God focuses on character. Let's suppose there are two men named John and Bill. Neither man steals. Society labels them honest. Yet there are two entirely different attitudes involved here. John won't steal because it goes against his nature. The thought of stealing nauseates him. Bill, on the other hand, doesn't steal because he is afraid of getting caught. That is the difference between confident, positive Christians and believers who aren't really happy followers of Christ.

Dedicated Christians give God the time He needs to build His Son's character into them, and that may be a painful and lengthy ordeal.

Even Jesus understood the process. "Though he were a Son, yet learned he obedience by the things which he suffered" (Heb. 5:8). As a matter of fact, Jesus struggled with doing the will of the Father right up to His last few days on earth. "And he was withdrawn from them about a stone's cast, and kneeled down, and prayed, Saying, Father, if thou be willing, remove this cup from me: nevertheless not my will, but thine, be done" (Luke 22:41-42). He knew the cross was inescapable, but His flesh recoiled at the thought. Still, He yielded to the Father's will, and by simple obedience He overcame the world. "In the world ye shall have tribulation: but be of good cheer; I have overcome the world" (John 16:33).

Notice He said, "I have overcome the world," *before* He was crucified. We don't have to wait to be overcomers.

There are many crosses in the life of the believer. Enlightened Christians understand the cross and its necessary work in their lives. I belonged to the unenlightened crowd. I thought it would be easy to follow Jesus. To add to the confusion, I thought the Lord made a marvelous choice when He saved me. It didn't take me long to realize God got the worst end of the deal. The blood certainly washed away all my sins, but I didn't know I needed the daily work of the cross. Self was still very much alive.

You won't ever overcome self, nor will you master it. The cross is the only remedy. Include it in your morning ritual. Brush your teeth, comb your hair, get dressed, turn on your cell phone, and take up your cross.

HOME, SWEET HOME

Do you remember a few years ago when pet pigs were popular? As a young evangelist, I explained the difficulty with the flesh by telling the story of a family who decided to domesticate a pig. They gleefully went to the pigsty and chose a tiny piglet just weaned from its mother. After a nice bath and some talcum powder, they dressed their newly adopted family member in navy blue shorts and a white shirt, accessorized with a red bow tie. Everything was fine until someone left the screen door unlatched. Out went piggy. They caught up with the little tyke rolling on its back in a big, yucky mud hole. As they approached the disheartening scene, they swore they heard the pig singing, "Home, sweet home!"

You won't change the flesh and you won't overcome it. Your flesh, your selfish nature, doesn't need reformation—it needs crucifixion. The Holy Spirit will take care of that if you let Him. Take up your cross daily and let it be your constant reminder. Faith is not about you—it's about Him. Faith is not about you becoming a spiritual powerhouse; it is hearing God say, "My grace is sufficient for thee, for my strength is made perfect in [your] weakness" (2 Cor. 12:9).

TODAY'S CROSS IS NEW AND IMPROVED

The old, rugged cross is nearly a forgotten element in the lives of believers. Today's cross is new and improved. We sand it down to a smooth finish. Then we tint it—not with blood, but with oak or maple stain. Lastly, we apply a nice coat of varnish and hang it above the baptistery. I'm not against a beautiful cross to complement church décor, but it seems we have somehow lost track of the true meaning of crucifixion. I shared the following thoughts in a single-adult meeting years ago and two elderly women got up and left the room. They misunderstood where I was going. I wasn't attacking the cross; I was attacking the traditional attitude we have toward the cross.

For instance, if Jesus had died in Gainesville, Georgia, in 1935, the Bible would read differently in certain places. This may sound strange, but I mean no disrespect. Crucifixion was the popular method of lethal punishment in Jesus' day. In the twentieth century, Scripture might read, "I have been strapped into an electric chair with Christ: nevertheless I live; yet not I, but Christ liveth in me" (Gal. 2:20). Depending on the era, the Christian symbol might be a guillotine, a hangman's noose, or even a gas chamber.

Political correctness has whitewashed the stigma of the old, rugged cross. Today, when we hear the word *cross,* we think of a jeweler. In Paul's day, the word *cross* made folks think of a jailor. I wonder how anxious we would be to hang a gold chain around our neck with an electric chair charm. Ultimately, the cross was a simple, yet crude, method of executing criminals. Thus the Bible talks about the shame of the cross. "Looking unto Jesus the author and finisher of our faith; who for the joy that was set before him endured the cross, *despising the shame,* and is set down at the right hand of God" (Heb. 12:2, emphasis mine). Christ died as a common criminal. The cross has a single purpose—execution. I like Marshall's translation of Galatians 2:20, "I have been co-crucified with Christ."

In other words, when He died, I died. *Less of me, Lord Jesus, and more of You,* should be our constant prayer. The Holy Spirit will use the cross to fulfill our request.

Just remember one thing. If you find the courage to pray that fateful prayer, "Lord, let the power of the cross work in me," be sure to fasten your spiritual seatbelt and get ready for a bumpy ride. You have probably had some cross experiences and didn't realize it. Fortunately, the end result will be glorious. Christ will be preeminent, and trusting Him will become second nature.

Also, know there will be spiritual scars. Your pride will die, your reputation may suffer and your desire to be in control will melt away. Never fear; resurrection life is glorious. It is His way, and it is the best of all ways.

There is an easier way, but it is empty and fruitless. Jesus said, "Enter by the narrow gate; for the gate is wide and the way is broad that leads to destruction, and many are those who enter by it. For the gate is small, and the way is narrow that leads to life, and few are those who find it" (Mt. 7:13–14 NASB).

Take up your cross and walk the narrow path with the man from Galilee. It is your calling. Embrace the cross, protect it, and cherish it. Just beyond the cross, resurrection life awaits. On the resurrection side of Calvary, there are no limits on what God can do through you.

Chapter 3

JOB HAD AN *I* PROBLEM

Not I, but Christ (Galatians 2:20)

The patience of Job has been a favorite sermon topic for centuries. I accepted the traditional view that portrayed Job as a very patient man. He certainly exhibited amazing patience in the early chapters of his book. Chapter one tells the painful story of the rustling of Job's oxen and asses by the Sabeans, the loss of his flocks of sheep, the death of his servants, the theft of his camels by the Chaldeans, and the agonizing, fatal loss of his sons and daughters. In response to losing virtually everything, "Job arose and tore his robe and shaved his head, and he fell to the ground and worshipped. And he said, 'Naked I came from my mother's womb, And naked I shall return there. The Lord gave and the Lord has taken away. Blessed be the name of the Lord.' Through all this Job did not sin nor did he blame God" (Job 1:20-22 NASB).

God's estimation of Job before his devastating experience was notable. "Again there was a day when the sons of God came to present themselves before the Lord, and Satan also came among them to present himself before the Lord" (Job 2:1 NASB). Verse 3 says, "And the Lord said to Satan, 'Have you considered My servant Job? For there is no one like him on the earth, a blameless and upright man fearing God and turning away from evil. And he still holds fast his integrity, although you incited Me against him, to ruin him without cause.'"

Tradition views Job's integrity and determination as extraordinary patience. But patience, in Job's case, had a limited warranty.

Over the years, I began to suspect Job's patience was not as enduring as I first imagined. Chinks in his armor began to show when God allowed Satan to attack Job physically. However, God drew the line when He said, "Behold, he is in thine hand; but save [spare] his life" (Job 2:6). Satan's plan was severe. "So went Satan forth from the presence of the Lord, and smote Job with sore boils from the sole of his foot unto his crown" (Job 2:7).

Job held his ground when his wife encouraged him to "curse God, and die" (v. 9). "But he said to her, 'You speak as one of the foolish women speaks. Shall we indeed accept good from God and not accept adversity?' In all this Job did not sin with his lips" (Job 2:10 NASB). So far, so good. His patience still sustained him.

Three of Job's friends heard of his affliction and came to mourn with him and comfort him. As they approached, the Bible says, "When they lifted up their eyes at a distance, and did not recognize him, they raised their voices and wept." (Job 2:12 NASB). The boils had so ravaged Job's body, even his close friends weren't sure it was him. Finally realizing it was Job and unprepared for his physical appearance, they showed their grief in true oriental fashion. They tore their clothes, perhaps the deepest expression of grief, and threw dust on their heads—an ancient reminder that God made man from the dust of the earth.

I WOULD HAVE THROWN IN THE TOWEL

Satan waited. He seemed to know Job's patience was more fleshly than Godly. Some people are blessed with a patient spirit. I am not one of them. Job's nature seemed to give him more than average patience, but all of us have a limit on our endurance for pain. Sure enough, Job broke after seven days. I would have thrown in the towel halfway through the first day. I'm being generous. With my low tolerance for pain, I may not have lasted the first hour. My wife spent over three years with a constant headache from a car accident, along with limited neck motion and endless nights of sleep deprivation. X-rays showed two crushed discs in her neck. Our chiropractor was amazed she could move her neck at all. I don't know how she stood it.

Why God waited so long is beyond us, but He instantly healed her one Sunday night as we fellowshipped with a minister friend and his wife. My friend prayed for her at the end of his message, and three years and six months of physical agony and frustration ended in a moment. She immediately had full range of motion in her neck and that night she slept like a baby for ten hours or more. She hadn't done that since the accident. Three hours of sleep seemed to be her limit.

I got up from the computer as I wrote this chapter and asked my wife if there was one lesson she learned during those three and a half years. She immediately said, "Patience." After her miracle, an x-ray showed her formerly s-shaped neck to be in perfect alignment.

WHY DID I NOT DIE AT BIRTH?

As I said, Job broke. "Afterward Job opened his mouth and cursed the day of his birth. And Job said, Let the day perish on which I was to be born" (Job 3:1-3 NASB). He goes on for several verses in the same negative vein. Verse 11 epitomized his frustration when he cried, "Why did I not die at birth, Come forth from the womb and expire?" He could no longer endure his grief and pain.

God was going for the ultimate lesson: "Trust Me, no matter what." However, God had some digging and rooting out to do first. Job's "I" problem quickly surfaces in his negative attitude. His words justify and, at the same time, betray him. "Then Job replied, Even today my complaint is rebellion; His hand is heavy despite my groaning" (Job 23:1-2 NASB).

Job believed God was meting out judgment with a heavy hand. The Lord had something else in mind.

Job continued his complaint—and then seemed to come to his senses. With his patience shredded, Job refused to surrender his faith. He said, "He knows the way that I take; When He has tried me, I shall come forth as gold" (Job 23:10 NASB). For all practical purposes, Job was learning to trust God with reckless abandon.

That is the true meaning of faith. After losing everything—his flocks, his children, and now his health—he trusted his life to God. I know pure persistence alone is not faith, but when it's all said and done, Job was one determined man.

Can you and I dare be that committed? I'd like to think so. With all hope gone, Job still wouldn't let go of God. In the end, patience should mesh with persistence until we can't tell one from the other.

As the chapter title suggests, Job had an *I* problem. In my mind, the lesson in the Book of Job is not patience. It is, rather, all about who's in charge. If we want to run our own lives, God will politely step back and let us do the driving. Somebody said, "You serve God in your way, and I'll serve God in my way." The problem is, if you serve God in your way and I serve God in my way, pretty soon there's nobody left to serve God in *His* way.

God's way is straight and narrow. Simply put, if selfishness is your master, the broad way is more attractive. You can walk there and still be in charge, brimming with fleshly self-confidence. The narrow way requires giving up your right to self-rule. After a lifetime of living for yourself, that can be scary.

WHAT ABOUT ME?

Job's real problem surfaces in chapter 29. In twenty-five short verses, Job refers to himself no less than fifty-two times. That's at least twice each verse. Job was still basically looking out for himself. Everything was still about him. His life revolved around the common cliché, "What about me?"

We don't know how much time passed during Job's trial, but the outcome was God-ordained. God's purpose in dealing with Job so severely became clear in the last chapter when Job confessed, "I have heard of thee by the hearing of the ear: but now mine eye seeth thee. Wherefore I abhor myself, and repent in dust and ashes" (Job 42:5-6). God was finally in charge of Job's life. Self-rule surrendered to Divine guidance. Job's heart became God's throne room.

I hope you can take comfort in Job's experience. Some tend to blame God for hard times. Worse yet, we often blame ourselves for poor choices or wrong decisions that bring unpleasant consequences. Yet God can take even our poor choices and use them to accomplish His purpose.

He used David's adulterous affair with Bath-sheba to bring Solomon into the world and, as a direct result, continued the lineage of Christ. He used jealous, conniving brothers who put Joseph's life in peril, but God turned it to save many lives during a terrible drought and famine in Egypt. God used Moses' poor judgment to gain the forty years needed to transform a shepherd into a leader He could use to deliver the entire nation of Israel. He used Peter's public denial of Christ to transform an angler into an apostle.

He can use our failures and even our sins, if need be, to build His character into us. If you are wondering why the promises of God are taking so long, wonder no more. God needs seasoned, selfless servants who never ask, "What about me?"

God restored everything to Job after his heart was renovated. Job's focus shifted away from self to God. God replaced self with Himself. "And the Lord turned the captivity of Job, when he prayed for his friends: also the Lord gave Job twice as much as he had before" (Job 42:10). I don't believe God turned Job's captivity *because* he prayed for his friends. Quite the contrary. Because God changed his heart, Job was, at last, free to focus on others. He stopped thinking about himself and that took a lengthy, divine adjustment.

TO DENY YOURSELF YOU MUST LEARN TO FORGET YOURSELF

Jesus reminds us, "Whosoever will come after me, let him deny himself, and take up his cross, and follow me" (Mark 8:34). To deny yourself, you must learn to forget yourself and your own interests, daring to believe God's interests are more important than yours. There are ways that seem right, and then there are God's ways. May the Holy Spirit teach us to know the difference and choose wisely.

Knowing the cross was part of His future, Jesus could have tiptoed away from the Garden of Gethsemane in the middle of the night and never been heard from again. We would never have been the wiser. He chose to do the Father's will. He kept to the course the Father laid out for Him. Christ knew the cross was inevitable, yet He found the courage to walk that most narrow of ways with joy. He looked beyond the short-term agony and embraced the victory that lay ahead. We are now reaping the benefits of His selfless life.

It was not a sin for Jesus to recoil at the prospect of dying on the cross. It is not a sin for us to wish there was an easier way to do the Father's will. We see the potential pain. God wants us to see the glory that will follow.

The writer of Hebrews reminds us to look "unto Jesus the author and finisher of our faith; who for the joy that was set before him endured the cross, despising the shame, and is set down at the right hand of the throne of God" (Heb. 12:2). Christ's journey intersected with Golgotha's cross. Our journey follows the same path. There is no other way. Embrace the cross and follow the Crucified One. Resurrection life beckons us. I'm not talking about life in heaven some day. I'm talking about abundant, victorious living right here, right now.

Stop waiting for victory. Start walking in it today! Say with Paul: "Thanks be to God, who gives us the victory through our Lord Jesus Christ" (1 Cor. 15:57 NASB). According to Bullinger, victory here means "conquest, *especially* victory in battle." Simply put, the spiritual warfare Paul emphasized is a conflict we are destined to win.

Chapter 4

FAITH MAKES YOU A TARGET

For the wind was contrary (Matthew 14:24)

My good friend Doug told me years ago, "Never forget you have an adversary." Satan hates believers for many reasons. Jesus made that abundantly clear. "And ye shall be hated of all men for my name's sake: but he that endureth to the end shall be saved" (Mt. 10:22). In His classic prayer to the Father, Jesus said, "I have given them thy word; and the world hath hated them, because they are not of the world, even as I am not of the world" (John 17:14).

Why are we hated? There is one simple reason—darkness hates light. "And this is the condemnation [judgment], that light is come into the world, and men loved darkness rather than light, because their deeds were evil" (John 3:19). Faith always faces contrary winds of popular opinion, in and outside the church. Those who choose to follow God fully will often have a lonely journey.

One thing never changes. Darkness always hates light, and those who love darkness cannot help hating what you stand for. The modern church seems hungry for worldly acceptance. The folly of political correctness has infected us. We are ever so careful not to offend anyone from the pulpit. If Christ had listened to popular opinion, He might have avoided that awful crucifixion. Of course, we would still be lost in our sins, living in spiritual poverty, and headed nowhere except into a dark eternity without God. Paul describes the lost as "having no hope, and without God in the world" (Eph. 2:12). If Christ had not died, we would all share that hopelessness.

Before introducing me as guest on a local Christian television program, the host related his disappointment because a listener objected to remarks he made on a previous telecast. When I sat down with him, he asked what I thought about the criticism. I said, "Welcome to the Kingdom of God, Jim."

I reminded him of Jesus' first public appearance in His hometown of Nazareth. "And he came to Nazareth, where he had been brought up: and, as his custom was, he went into the synagogue and stood up for to read. And there was delivered unto him the book of the prophet Esaias [Isaiah]" (John 4:16). Christ read Isaiah 61:1-2, verses that describe the Messiah to come. He concluded with the fateful words, "This day is this scripture fulfilled in your ears" (Luke 4:21). Realizing Christ had just claimed to be the Messiah, the members of the synagogue became violent. "And all they in the synagogue, when they heard these words, were filled with wrath, And rose up, and thrust him out of the city, and led him unto the brow of the hill whereon their city was built, that they might cast him down headlong" (Luke 4:28-29). After speaking less than two hundred words, angry Jewish leaders promptly threw Christ out of the synagogue.

The fuming crowd, not satisfied with expelling Him from the building, proceeded to chase Him down to throw Him off a cliff. "But he passing through the midst of them went his way" (Luke 4:30). On that day, light survived the hatred of darkness.

THE WORLD HAS NEVER BEEN OUR MODEL

Society says, "Give me, amuse me, feed me, soothe me, serve me, pleasure me, help me," and the list goes on. The world has never been our model, yet the Church seems willing to do whatever it takes to grow numerically with less and less consideration for the spiritual validity of the method. The simple gospel of Jesus Christ is no longer enough for some.

Henry M. Morris, Ph.D., was an early creationist who wrote several books exposing the unscientific basis of evolution. He had the opportunity to debate with evolutionists numerous times at various universities in America. He handily won his debates using scientific arguments alone. Invariably, a number of college students sought him out after each debate to learn more about Christ and the Bible. Dr. Morris said he never used science with the inquiring students. He simply told them the old story of the cross and each time the Holy Spirit drew a number of students to accept Christ.

What spirit is pressing us today to use any method we can think of to attract people to church? The Holy Spirit, according to Christ Himself, has one purpose. Jesus said, "He shall glorify me" (John 16:14). The Holy Spirit will induce us to glorify the Father and the Son. Jesus said, "And whatsoever ye shall ask in my name, that will I do, that the Father may be glorified in the Son" (John 14:13).

Christ should have the final word about church methodology. "And I, if I be lifted up from the earth, will draw all men unto me." (John 12:32). He referred to His imminent death on the cross. Paul was clear when he said, "And I, brethren, when I came to you, came not with excellency of speech or of wisdom, declaring unto you the testimony of God. For I determined not to know any thing among you, save Christ, and him crucified" (1 Cor. 2:1-2).

Never forget, His blood stained the ground beneath that old rugged cross. He had every right to be offended. Instead, He asked His Father to forgive the offenders as they drove the nails. When nothing else is working in the church to draw the lost, why don't we just try talking about the crucified One?

I still love the church—with its denominational divisions, its doctrinal differences, and its myriad of faith declarations. I don't like what divides us and I doubt we'll ever be free of the cobwebs of tradition that narrow our views.

RELIGION IS MAN'S IDEA

I have a friend who took a university course titled "World Religions." The first day, the professor invited students to crowd around his desk. With everyone leaning in to hear, the instructor said, "Let's make one thing perfectly clear. This is a course in religion—it has *nothing* to do with God." He reminded his students that religion is man's idea and, far too often, religion makes little room for God.

Somewhere in the midst of the Church of Jesus Christ, we desperately need to hear John the Baptist declare, "Behold the Lamb of God, who takes away the sin of the world" (John 1:29 NASB). Christ must be the beginning, the middle, and the end of everything we believe and practice, or we will be off-center. "I am Alpha and Omega, the beginning and the ending, saith the Lord, which is, and which was, and which is to come, the Almighty" (Rev. 1:8).

I personally believe nothing troubles Satan more than a Christian who understands the centrality of Christ. When we declare Christ as the only solution to man's condition, the Father can do what He loves. "No man can come to me," Jesus said, "except the Father which hath sent me draw him: and I will raise him up at the last day" (John 6:44). He alone draws men.

Will the simple preaching of the cross attract unbelievers to Christ? Yes, it will, if we remember Paul's words: "And He is before all things, and in Him all things hold together. He is also head of the body, the church; and He is the beginning, the firstborn from the dead; so that He Himself will come to have first place in everything" (Col. 1:17-18 NASB).

There's good news and there's bad news. When we find the courage to preach Christ and Him crucified, that simple message will attract the lost like nothing else. That's the good news. What's the bad news? When we preach Christ and Him crucified, the world will once again hate us as they hated Him. Nevertheless, the truth of the cross will reach hearts if we dare preach it without coveting man's approval.

PREACHING A BENIGN, INOFFENSIVE GOSPEL IS SAFE

The Holy Spirit spoke through James in uncompromising terms when he said, "Do you not know that friendship with the world is hostility toward God? Therefore whoever wishes to be a friend of the world makes himself an enemy of God" (James 4:4 NASB). Preaching a benign, inoffensive Gospel is safe and it has its advantages. Satan will not oppose us so much and the world just might accept us as an okay bunch of folks. On the other hand, Jesus said, "Woe unto you, when all men shall speak well of you!" (Luke 6:26).

We have a clear path to walk. Christ commands us, "Go ye therefore, and teach all nations" (Mt. 28:19). The Christian church was birthed on the day of Pentecost with the fulfilled promise of Christ: "But ye shall receive power, after that the Holy Ghost is come upon you: and ye shall be witnesses unto me both in Jerusalem [your home town], and in all Judaea [throughout your state], and in Samaria [your country], and unto the uttermost part of the earth" (Acts 1:8).

In the process of obeying Christ's command to evangelize, we should never be guilty of intentional antagonism. Don't be a religious weirdo on the job, for instance. I had a friend who lost her job because she couldn't resist correcting coworkers with Scripture when they misspoke or showed an inappropriate attitude.

Public opinion won't come against us as often if we use wisdom. Instead of showing disapproval for coworkers' conversations or behavior, quietly become the best worker on the payroll. Be on time, work conscientiously, and be a helper instead of a religious nuisance. Eventually, fellow employees will notice your peaceful spirit and uncompromising moral fiber. You will have abundant opportunities to be a blessing and encouragement. Christians who quietly bide their time in the workplace will be sought out for advice by coworkers who really need answers when difficult times come. You have the answer. His name is Jesus.

The world is consistently asking for help. No one is going to walk up and say, "Tell me about the God who makes you like you are." If you listen closely, however, you can hear pleas for help.

A man asked me one day if I had a cigarette. I said, "No sir, I don't smoke."

He said, "Man, I wish I had that habit."

I'm guilty of singing in public. People often comment, "You sure are happy." They are saying, "I'm not that happy; what's your secret?" I don't mind telling them how good the Lord is to me.

LET YOUR LIGHT SHINE—NOT YOUR SPOTLIGHT

People today are looking for truth. Because of spiritual blindness, many look in the wrong place. Paul helps us here. "But if our gospel be hid, it is hid to them that are lost: In whom the god of this world hath blinded the minds of them which believe not, lest the light of the glorious gospel of Christ, who is the image of God, should shine unto them" (2 Cor. 4:3-4). To His followers, Christ says, "Let your light so shine before men, that they may see your good works, and glorify your Father which is in heaven" (Mt. 5:16). Take Jesus' advice and let your light shine—*not* your spotlight.

In other words, don't point out people's faults; show them what the Gospel looks like lived out in everyday life.

In Matthew, Christ suggested a single candlestick can provide light for everyone in a house. "Neither do men light a candle, and put it under a bushel [basket], but on a candlestick; and it giveth light unto all that are in the house" (Mt. 5:15). When we practice silence, the light of our spirit pierces the darkness. The peace of Christ in our hearts will permeate any atmosphere. When the opportunity arises, you can share your faith. Your time to shine for Christ will come.

There are facts in Scripture we would rather not discuss. The early church saw incredible miracles. They also experienced severe persecution. Preaching Christ often comes with a price. If you expect to declare the truth of Christ and His cross without opposition, or without ruffling anyone's feathers, you will taste disappointment. If you dare to preach Christ and Him crucified, public opinion may come against you, but those who hear the truth of your testimony and embrace it will be eternally grateful—and heaven will rejoice.

I'M SURE PAUL BIT HIS LIP AT TIMES

Only the Holy Spirit can guide us as we walk this spiritual tightrope. May we have a sensitive ear and learn when to talk and when to be quiet. The Spirit of Christ drove Paul to preach the Gospel. "Woe is me, if I do not preach the gospel" (1 Cor. 9:16 NASB). The Holy Spirit gave him tremendous wisdom in the effort. "For though I am free from all men, I have made myself a slave to all that I might win the more.

And to the Jews I became as a Jew, that I might win Jews; to those who are under the Law, as under the Law . . . that I might win those who are under the Law; to those who are without law, as without law . . . that I might win those who are without law. To the weak I became weak, that I might win the weak; I have become all things to all men, that I may by all means save some" (1 Cor. 9:19–22 NASB).

I'm sure Paul bit his lip at times when he wanted to respond harshly to those he ministered to. May the Holy Spirit teach us when to bite our lip and when to speak the truth. Solomon affirmed this simple rule when he said there is "a time to keep silence, and a time to speak" (Eccl. 3:7). Holy Spirit, give us wisdom—and teach us patience.

MONTHS OF PATIENCE PAID OFF

As a public school teacher, I could never initiate a conversation with a student about faith or religion. I could respond to student questions, however, and often did. One year, I had a high school senior who privately expressed his frustration with church and he eventually told me he didn't believe in God at all. I kept my silence. Finally, the last day of school, he approached me after his final exam in history. All my other students were gone. He opened the door by asking a question about faith. Months of patience paid off. I shared with him from my heart, encouraging him to keep an open mind toward God. He wasn't ready to accept Christ, but he heard me. I trust the Holy Spirit has kept this young man's mind open to Christ.

Be led by the Spirit to witness, but don't be surprised if He restrains you to be quiet at times. He knows who is receptive and who isn't. Be bold, but don't be antagonistic. Remember: faith makes you a target. Follow the Holy Spirit's lead and fewer arrows will come your way, but never forget you have an adversary. The more you focus on Christ and

Him crucified, the more the enemy will oppose you—and the more the Holy Spirit will anoint you.

Satan knows the blood of Christ has made him terminally weak and he hates us for it. "What shall we then say to these things?" Paul asks. "If God be for us, who can be against us?" (Rom. 8:31). Well, let me think. The world is against us. Sometimes our own families are against us. Liberal media bias is against us. Evolutionary theory is against us. Popular opinion is against us. Everybody and everything can be against us, but nothing will change God's mind. He's on our side, no matter what.

"Who can be against us?" Paul asks in Romans 8:31. Then he answers his own question. "Who shall separate us from the love of Christ? shall tribulation, or distress, or persecution, or famine, or nakedness, or peril, or sword? As it is written, For thy sake we are killed all the day long; we are accounted as sheep for the slaughter. Nay, in all these things we are more than conquerors through him that loved us" (Rom. 8:35-37).

How can we be more than conquerors? I have a theory. We have an adversary, but the fight was fixed "before the foundation of the world" (Eph. 1:4). Revelation 13:8 refers to "the book of life of the Lamb slain from the foundation of the world." God provided reconciliation for everyone before He created Adam and Eve. The sacrifice of Christ was a finished work in the mind of the Father, Son and Holy Spirit before the first breath of creation.

WE CANNOT AND WILL NOT LOSE THE WAR

Like it or not, we are engaged in spiritual warfare. We may lose a skirmish here or there, but we cannot and will not lose the war. To be sure, enemy arrows will come our way. May David's prayer be ours: "Thou art my hiding place and my shield: I hope in thy word" (Ps. 119:114). Simple faith will embolden you to face the opposition of public opinion and make sure Satan's darts don't penetrate your backside.

By the way, arrows in your hind parts suggest retreat. For too long, we have unwittingly assumed a position of defense against Satan and his demonic forces. Scripture gives no reason to take a defensive posture. When an army is on the defense, it is far too easy to retreat if the battle becomes too severe. The Bible never assumes or even hints at a Church on the defense. The words of an old hymn fit here—"Like a mighty army moves the Church of God." What did earlier believers know that we seem to have forgotten, if indeed, we knew it in the first place? The next chapter suggests one possible answer.

Chapter 5

THE GATES OF HELL ARE STATIONARY

And He said Come (Matthew 14:29)

With a severe storm threatening to swamp the small band of disciples, Christ finally came to their aid. Peter, seeing Him, said, "Lord, if it be thou, bid me come unto thee on the water."

Without hesitation, Jesus said, "Come."

Jesus talked a lot about the Church playing offense instead of defense. Offense means action. It means forward motion. It means charging into the fray—or, in Peter's case, stepping onto stormy waves with no tangible footing. Much like an army, the early Church stayed on the offense.

Armies have a singular goal: advance into enemy territory and occupy. Recently, a minister friend from the old school expressed disapproval of the militant tone of worship songs we often hear in the Church today. I reminded him of Paul's declarations, "Fight the good fight of faith" (1 Tim. 6:12), "I have fought a good fight" (2 Tim. 4:7), "The weapons of our warfare are not carnal, but mighty through God to the pulling down of [demonic] strong holds" (2 Cor. 10:4).

This chapter's title, *THE GATES OF HELL ARE STATIONARY,* is taken from Jesus' words to Peter: "Thou art Peter, and upon this rock I will build My church; and the gates of hell shall not prevail against it" (Mt. 16:18).

The unique thing I missed for years about the gates of hell is the fact that gates are stationary. They don't move. They don't gain ground; they hold ground. Gates don't have feet; they have footers, or foundations. Gates have a two-fold purpose: forbid admittance and deny exit. Gates generally protect property from intruders.

Satan has taken a lot of ground from the Church—we need to take it back. It is time to intrude.

The story of Jericho parallels our theme. "Now Jericho was straitly shut up because of the Children of Israel: none went out and none came in" (Josh. 6:1). Jericho was directly in the Israelites' path as they marched into the promised land. The Israelites had one problem with the city of Jericho: the gates were shut tight and virtually impenetrable.

Unger's Bible Dictionary tells us Jericho had double walls made of brick. The outer wall was six feet thick and twelve to fifteen feet high. The inner wall stood fifteen feet from the outer wall. It was twelve feet thick and about thirty feet high, with apartments built into it. It resembled a three-story apartment building.

Rahab, a resident of Jericho, entertained and hid the two spies Joshua had sent only a few days earlier to scope out the city. They escaped Jericho when she "let them down by a cord through the window: for her house was upon the town wall, and she dwelt upon the wall" (Josh. 2:15).

Archeological research indicates the outer walls fell away from the city and the inner walls fell outward as well, with debris filling the fifteen-foot space between them. Archeologists provide no explanation.

HOW QUICKLY WE FORGET YESTERDAY'S MIRACLE IN THE FACE OF TODAY'S TRIAL

With Jericho's walls intact, the foreboding obstacle loomed before Israel. What did God tell the Israelites to do?

Walk around the city once a day for six days. That's it. That made about as much sense as believing God to part water just by striking it with a stick, which is exactly what happened forty years earlier at the Red Sea. How quickly we forget yesterday's miracle in the face of today's trial.

To make matters worse, God told Joshua to instruct the people to keep their mouths shut as they marched. "Ye shall not shout, nor make any noise with your voice, neither shall any word proceed out of your mouth, until the day I bid you shout; then shall ye shout" (Josh. 6:10).

Few things provoke believers more than God insisting they do something that makes no sense at all, and do it without saying a word or making the slightest sound. Then, for reasons no one could fathom, God instructed Joshua to tell the priests to blow with the trumpets every step of the way as they marched around the city. I won't even guess what went through their minds as every Israelite—man, woman and child—walked in silence to blaring trumpets and mocking Jerichoites.

To their credit, the Israelites swallowed their pride and followed Joshua's orders. After nearly a week of daily orbits around the city, Joshua gave the final day's instructions. Israel will march around the city—not once, but seven times. Off they went for seven additional laps with no expected tangible results. They obediently finished their final lap, accompanied with trumpets that, by now, must have become very irritating.

As the last Israelite crossed the finish line, Joshua declared, "Shout; for the Lord hath given you the city" (Josh. 6:16).

I can imagine they looked at each in stunned silence and thought in unison, "What good will that do?" Eventually, the first brave Israelite (probably a child) let out the first whimper of a shout. One by one, they joined the meager chorus. I can hear the growing sound rippling until it rivals the roar of the crowd on Super Bowl Sunday.

The younger Israelites may have forgotten the simple principle of faith established forty years earlier as their predecessors stood at the Red Sea. Blocked from going forward by an impassable body of water and flanked by the pursuing army of Egyptians, Moses spoke words that make trusting God the sanest and safest course we could ever follow. "Fear ye not, stand still, and see the salvation of the Lord, which he will shew to you today . . . The Lord shall fight for you, and ye shall hold your peace" (Ex. 14:13-14).

As the weary marchers began to obey Joshua's command to shout, I can imagine an unexplained tremor coming from deep underground. Scripture is silent on such details, but tells us, "and it came to pass, when the people heard the sound of the trumpet, and the people shouted with a great shout, that the wall fell down flat, so that the people went up into the city, every man straight before him, and they took the city" (Josh. 6:20).

"And it came to pass" is a phrase found throughout Scripture. I counted nearly fifty mentions of that phrase in the book of Genesis alone. Those ominous words precede nearly every promise of God about to come to fruition. If God says, "It's going to rain," you'd best build an ark—or, at least, find an umbrella and some high boots.

Before leaving the story of Jericho, I'd like to share something I noticed one day as I read the eleventh chapter of Hebrews, often referred to as the "faith chapter" by Bible commentators. It has to do, not with what is there, but with what is missing entirely from that concise history of the Israelites. Many teach the Old Testament to be a time of justification by obedience to the law. Yet, according to the writer of Hebrews, it has to do with faith and faith alone.

"By faith Abraham . . . by faith Isaac . . . by faith Jacob . . . by faith Joseph . . . by faith Moses" (Heb. 11:17-24). Verse 29 says, "By faith they passed through the Red Sea as by dry land: which the Egyptians assaying to do were drowned."

Verse 30 continues, "By faith the walls of Jericho fell down, after they were compassed about seven days."

Wait a minute, I said to myself. Between verse 29 and verse 30, the writer says nothing about the forty years of Israel's wilderness wanderings. Why is that episode missing? Those four decades of unbelief don't belong in the chapter of faith.

RECIPE FOR REVIVAL

The story of Israel in the wilderness reveals a serious obstacle to faith. Years ago, God whispered in my ear and said, "I'm going to give you a recipe for revival." He immediately followed with a verse I had read many times: "Do all things without murmurings and disputings" (Phil. 2:14). That didn't sound very exciting, but when I studied the two words—"murmurings" and "disputings"—it became clear. According to Bullinger, "murmur" means "to complain or manifest discontent" and "dispute" means "to investigate jointly to express your opinion."

You can complain all by yourself. "Disputing" requires group participation. In other words, complainers can murmur alone, but when they illicit the opinion of others, it becomes disputing. An Israelite in the wilderness could say to himself, "I don't like the direction Moses is taking us." He is murmuring or just complaining. To make his complaining an act of disputing he only needs to ask someone, "What do you think?" That question turns complainers into disputers and possibly explains Israel's forty-year circular journey in the wilderness.

Murmuring can make you miserable. Disputing drags others into your misery and can have drastic consequences on their lives. The writer of Hebrews warned of the potential damage when he admonished us to "Follow peace with all men, and holiness, without which no man shall see the Lord:

Looking diligently lest any man fail of the grace of God; lest any root of bitterness springing up trouble you, and thereby many be defiled" (Heb. 12:14–15).

The same complaining that barred Israel from entering the promise land can lead to bitter church splits in the twenty-first century.

Complaining will block faith's flow immediately. Complainers focus on themselves and their own comfort and pleasure. Drawing someone else into your discontentment is the first step in starting division. No one can cause a church split by himself—he needs disciples.

COMPLAINING CHOKES FAITH

The Holy Spirit emphatically declares through Paul, "Do all things *without* murmurings and disputings" (emphasis mine). When it comes to complaining and division, the Holy Spirit warns, "Don't do it!" Complaining chokes faith. Don't complain—but, if you feel you must, keep it to yourself. Never solicit others to agree with you.

The solution is simple—it is difficult to complain if you focus on Christ. If we can learn to resist the luxury of complaining, disputing won't come into play and faith can flourish individually and corporately. If you dislike the atmosphere in your church, work prayerfully and lovingly to improve it. If that doesn't work, leave quietly and leave alone. There may be nothing wrong with the atmosphere at your church. It may be time for you to admit, *It's me, it's me, oh Lord, standin' in the need of prayer.*

The Jericho episode was an early example of God teaching His people the principle of faith. We trust; God acts. We relax and He does the rest. Believing is our only work. Jesus confirmed that principle when He answered the disciples' question, "What shall we do that we may work the works of God?"

Jesus replied, "This is the work of God, that you believe in Him whom He has sent" (John 6:28-29 NASB).

Here is another paradox of Christianity. As explained earlier, we rest first and then act from a position of rest. The writer of Hebrews explains it beautifully, saying, "For we who have believed enter that rest" (Heb. 4:3 NASB). A few verses later, he explains, "There remaineth therefore a rest to the people of God. For he that is entered into his [God's] rest, he also hath ceased from his own works, as God did from his" (Heb. 4:9-10). There you have it. We walk in faith and God does the rest. Yes, He uses us and yes, we are always amazed when He does. The more we rest in faith, the more God acts. Go figure.

GOD WILL ALWAYS SHOW UP AND TAKE CARE OF BUSINESS

Faith is not effort; faith is trusting from a position of rest. Faith knows God will eventually come through, one way or another. You may face a sea blocking your march, a desert with no water, a fiery furnace, a den of lions, or a hundred other faith-crunching obstacles. You may have to march day after day with no visible results. You may have to live among ravenous lions, trek through a barren wilderness, or navigate stormy seas. Faith insists, *God will always show up and take care of business.*

Never forget that God knows where you are and where He wants to take you. He plans to get you there intact if you trust Him. That leads to one last question: Why did Israel wander in the wilderness for forty years?

Following the rule of simplicity, the writer of Hebrews answers our question: "So we see that they could not enter in because of their unbelief" (Heb. 3:19). Israel's complaining generated doubt and kept them from occupying and enjoying the land of promise. Complaining also stifles our God-given ability to believe. Unbelief renders us immobile and ineffective. Faith stirs us to assault Satan's gates without fear. The power of the Holy Spirit energizes us to be gatecrashers.

Jesus discussed the existence of the gates of hell and their ability to impede the progress of the church by giving us a lesson in geology. He said to Peter, "Thou art Peter, and upon this rock I will build my church; and the gates of hell shall not prevail against it" (Mt. 16:18). Peter's name in the Greek is *pétros:* "a rolling stone, in one place today and another tomorrow" (Bullinger). Jesus used the word "rock" *(pétra),* from the same root as *pétros,* but with a difference worth noting. According to Bullinger, *pétros* is a small stone that might be thrown by hand. *Pétra,* on the other hand, is the same material, but not the same size or makeup. It denotes a cliff or a huge boulder.

When Jesus said, "On this rock I will build my church," he used the word *pétra.* That is the word Paul used to describe Christ as "that Rock" (1 Cor. 10:4). You and I become part of the Church structure itself. However, the true picture of the Church is not a stationary building, but a living body. Peter refers to believers as "living stones . . . built up as a spiritual house" (1 Pet. 2:5 NASB).

Keep in mind, the term "house" in Scripture almost always means family. After he became king, David said, "Is there yet any that is left of the house of Saul, that I may shew him kindness for Jonathan's sake?" (2 Sam. 9:1). The early church was a spiritual family on the move, a virtual army of fearless soldiers crashing through gates and taking land away from the enemy everywhere they went.

The intriguing thing about this story is the reference to the gates of hell. As I said earlier, gates don't move. The only way hell's gates can prevail against the Church is if we don't assault them. The Church today has seemingly adopted a defensive posture—a holding pattern, if you please. We tend to make great plans we seldom implement outside the four walls we call "church."

The possibility looms that the Church is, for the most part, content on holding the ground already taken, has circled the wagons and forgotten about going into the entire world to preach the Gospel. We occupied territory, built beautiful, spiritual bunkers, and now hope the lost will come looking for us because we are seeker-friendly and likeable. We cheerfully support foreign missionaries, yet tend to ignore the mission field around us where we quietly shop for groceries, buy gas, and take walks in our neighborhood.

That defensive mindset may be the result of the Church long ago adopting the Augustinian worldview that teaches something I have trouble embracing. Augustine, a fourth century theologian, taught what Gregory Boyd calls the "blueprint world view" in his outstanding book, *Satan and the Problem of Evil.* Augustine assumed there must be some divine purpose behind all evil deeds and every catastrophe. He believed everything that happens, good or bad, somehow fits into God's overall plan.

GOD TOOK A GREAT RISK

The early church, on the other hand, believed they lived in a spiritual war zone—and in war, terrible things happen to innocent people. The military calls it collateral damage. Augustine had trouble with that view because it seemed to suggest God wasn't in control and was not sovereign. He failed to include in the discussion, as Boyd suggests, the free will of man. God created man as a free agent capable of doing anything he wants, good or evil. God took a great risk when He chose to create beings with free will, as Satan's rebellion clearly reveals.

God wanted man to have the choice to love Him without coercion. Forced love is not real love. Irenaeus, an early

Church father, said, "There is no coercion with God." From before creation, God wanted a family of sons and daughters who would freely love Him without pressure. That also means those same individuals have the freedom to reject His love—and many do. It was the price God our Father was willing to pay so He could enjoy children who love Him by choice. Those who reject God's love are the indirect source of the evil, sordid things done to innocent people.

Satan, of course, is the original rebel and the inspiration behind the deeds of evil men. Planet Earth is a risky place to live. Bad things happen. It doesn't suggest the absence or weakness of God. It simply affirms the presence and influence of Satan, the original rebel.

Natural calamities such as floods, hurricanes, and earthquakes are also a result of the fall of Satan and the original disobedience of man. Paul called Satan, "the prince of the power of the air" (Eph. 2:2). Another sea story involves Jesus and His disciples getting into a small ship and heading out to sea. Scripture tells us a storm ensued and threatened their safety. The disciples woke the sleeping Master and said, "Save us, Lord; we are perishing!" And He said to them, "Why are you timid, you men of little faith?" Then He arose and rebuked the winds and the sea; and it became perfectly calm (Mt. 8:25-26 NASB).

The fact that Jesus "rebuked" the winds suggests that spiritual forces influenced them. Paul insists even the natural world is subject to the corrupting influence of Satan when he says, "The creature itself also shall be delivered from the bondage of corruption into the glorious liberty of the children of God. For we know that the whole creation groaneth and travaileth in pain until now. And not only they, but ourselves also, which have the firstfruits of the Spirit, even we ourselves groan within ourselves, waiting for the adoption, to wit, the redemption of our body" (Romans 8:21-23).

Everything on planet Earth is subject to the opposition of physical and spiritual agents. We need God's protection in every way. I believe God can and will intervene in our lives in direct response to Satan's interference. If we simply ask Him, God will move on our behalf and turn obstacles into opportunities. God used forty years of sheep herding to chisel Moses into a great leader. He used Joseph's betrayal by his brothers to turn into good what Satan intended for evil. Joseph told his brothers, "And as for you, you meant evil against me, but God meant it for good in order to bring about this present result, to preserve many people alive" (Gen. 50:20 NASB).

At the same time, if God interfered or intervened to keep bad things from happening, then man's free will is no longer free, but controlled somewhat by God. Any love from humans at that point is not freely given and the entire free will concept breaks down. The Church's adoption of Augustine's worldview moved believers from a position of offense to a hunker-down mentality and it seems we have maintained a defensive stance to this day.

POLITICAL CORRECTNESS HAS BECOME OUR ACHILLES' HEEL

We talk about the Christian's need to be bold, but I suspect the defensive mindset hinders us. We are disturbingly careful not to offend anyone with our witness. Political correctness has become our Achilles' heel—our soft spot. We are forgetting one thing: darkness will hate light either way. Souls are in jeopardy. Eternal separation from God is a real possibility for multitudes. We shouldn't be obnoxious or pushy when we share Christ. At the same time, let's not forget what Jesus did in the temple with a whip and a full head of righteous steam. He took action and physically drove dishonest religious leaders from the synagogue.

Are we going to sit idly by and let Satan steal our children's hearts and minds? Are we going to say, "It's all good" and believe it will eventually prove to be God's will? Can the assault and murder of a five-year-old girl and other unbelievably heinous acts somehow fit into God's plan? I refuse to believe it. It does fit into Satan's limited freedom to cause havoc on the earth. Could God stop him? Of course—and, at the appointed time, He will. Until then, men with free will can choose to love God or oppose Him, and God, our loving Father, allows that choice. That doesn't prove His weakness; it applauds His willingness to take an incredible risk in order to enjoy the freely given love of His children.

As I mentioned earlier, the early church believed they lived in a spiritual warzone. The warfare worldview they embraced doesn't answer all the questions about why bad things happen, but it answers most of them to my satisfaction. The Augustinian view tries to make everything part of God's will, but it leaves questions we can't answer and the world mocks us for it—questions that always start with, "How could a loving God allow such a tragedy?" That argument questions the very existence of God.

Our simple answer is the obvious presence of the original rebel, Satan, who darkens the hearts of the gullible and inspires them to do unspeakable things.

God's gift of free will requires Him to let nature take its course for the time being. Thus we see violence in the animal kingdom, as well as among men. Survival of the fittest has been the rule since the fall of man in the garden. The early church stormed the gates of hell and paid the price. Christ's enemies stoned Stephen, and according to tradition, boiled the apostle Peter in oil. John the Baptist was beheaded. Jesus was crucified. History documents the tens of thousands of Christians in the first and second centuries that were burned at the stake, fed to lions, or pulled apart by horses—just for sport.

We can't imagine that kind of persecution. Protected in our American culture by our Constitution and the wonderful freedoms it provides, we are shielded and coddled into a false sense of security.

Satan has had two thousand years to repair the damage the early church did to the gates of hell. Those fearless believers almost tore those gates off their hinges. We live in a world that openly resents us without reason, much the same as Palestinians hate Jews and don't know why. Christians are ridiculed in the cinema and media and, for some reason the world refuses to admit, we are attacked more than any other faith. The reason remains the same—darkness hates light, especially the light of the cross.

HE HATES US AND FOR GOOD REASON

Satan targets believers. He hates us for good reason. We have replaced him as the agent of praise to the Almighty. We are now the true worshippers of the Godhead. May we lift our voices in these last days until the very gates of hell vibrate with our ear-splitting praise and worship to God. My dear friend Randy Lechner is very loud when he praises God. Someone asked him one day, "Pastor, why are you so loud when you worship?" Randy answered, "Because it disarms the enemy."

Are we destined to become the generation of anemic, non-offensive believers Revelation 3:16 identifies as the "lukewarm" church in the last days? I pray we can avoid that label. The four-wall mentality of the modern church has made us aggressive worshippers in church and quiet, respectful, and nearly unnoticed citizens outside those hallowed walls.

I've heard Randy Lechner say, "The purpose of the church in America today is to go to church." The purpose of the early church was to go into the entire world. Is it going to take radical politicians threatening to take away our rights to wake us from our two thousand-year nap? Will persecution become necessary? Over the years, there have been renewals, awakenings, and revivals, but the defensive mindset always seems to creep back in.

Most of what we do for Christ happens inside the four walls of the church. I believe the Holy Spirit is anxious to free us from the shackles that confine us to a four-wall mentality.

Meanwhile, our mental conflict continues. Conflict occurs when our ideals and our reality are on two different levels. For instance, we believe, without apology, that miracles are possible, that they occurred on a regular basis in the early church, and they can and do still happen today in the lives of the faithful. The rarity of genuine miracles is the source of our mental conflict. The early believers were bold because they experienced the miraculous daily. They had a secret weapon. They focused on the Miracle Worker.

My friend Arthur Leis can relate to the early church. Listening to him share some of the creative miracles he saw during times of intense persecution in Africa stirs my spirit. In 1962, Idi Amin marched through Kenya and Uganda and slaughtered three hundred thousand people, many of them Christians. During that era of persecution, Arthur saw incredible miracles occur. At the time, there were only eight churches in Uganda as the result of Arthur's missionary efforts there. Idi Amin and his thugs slaughtered every man, woman, and child in six of those churches.

The violence was unbelievable. Among other things, Idi's soldiers cut open the stomachs of pregnant women and threw the unborn babies to crocodiles. Other believers discovered the atrocities when they followed the bloodstained water upstream. Arthur said, years later, human skulls of both children and adults were still being discovered on the river bottom in that area.

"Precious in the sight of the Lord is the death of His saints" (Ps. 116:15).

THE BOY HAD NO BONES IN HIS LEGS

As fellow Christians hand-dug graves in the sand to bury their slain brothers and sisters in Christ, miracles occurred days on end. Arthur shared the following story. A father had a young son he pushed around on a crude, one-wheeled cart. The boy had no bones in his legs. They flopped over the edge of the cart like a loose towel slung over a waiter's arm. The father pushed his son for miles to help bury his fellow slain Christians.

When he arrived, he set the cart down. Suddenly witnesses heard popping, crackling sounds. Arthur and the others stopped digging and looked toward the strange noises. They watched the boy's legs and feet straighten as God literally created bones before their very eyes. That young boy, only moments later, stood on those formerly useless legs and feet and walked for the first time in his life.

Arthur said the miracles were too numerous to recount. To this day, Christian descendants from those Ugandan churches refer to that era as the time "when heaven came close to the earth." May heaven come close to the earth in these last days.

One notable thing about the cruel reign of Idi Amin in Africa is the fact that God told Arthur it was coming and even showed him the specific route the ruthless dictator would take. He had opportunity to share that information with government leaders in Kenya. They scoffed and told Arthur it could never happen. It happened exactly as he predicted and innocent people suffered as a result. That courageous missionary said he longed to see miracles of that magnitude once again before he dies. I hope it won't require persecution.

We have enough faith. Perhaps if we stop asking for more and start expecting things to happen, they will. The gates of hell may challenge our faith, hinder our advance into enemy territory, and cause us mental conflict. Our walk may not equal our words, but Timothy reminds us, "God hath not given us a spirit of cowardice, but of power and love and self-control" (2 Tim. 1:7 Marshall).

Faith leads to miracles. Miracles spawn spiritual boldness and that boldness will shake the very gates of hell. We should also remember the words of Jesus: "Behold, I give unto you power to tread on serpents and scorpions, and over all the power of the enemy" (Luke 10:19).

The gates of hell are vulnerable to those of us who make Christ the center of everything we do and teach. Those gates, according to Christ, "will not prevail against the Church." Our modern church facilities are comfortable, but a suffering world waits, imprisoned behind those gates.

Jesus said, "I will give you the keys of the kingdom of heaven; and whatever you shall bind on earth shall be bound in heaven, and whatever you shall loose on earth shall be loosed in heaven" (Mt. 16:19 NASB). We have the keys. It is time we use them to set the captive free.

Chapter 6

JESUS—ALWAYS ON TIME

And in the fourth watch of the night Jesus went unto them (Matthew 14:25)

We live in time while God lives in eternity. We use calendars that show us a month at a glance. God's calendar is more like a decade at a glance. Consequently, we are time-conscious while God is eternity-conscious. We look at our watches and calendars; God just sees. "The eyes of the Lord are in every place, beholding the evil and the good" (Prov. 15:3). God knows what is happening in our lives. "For the eyes of the Lord move to and fro throughout the earth that He may strongly support those whose heart is completely His" (2 Chron. 16:9 NASB).

Have you noticed how seldom God does what we expect, much less the way we expect it? Furthermore, He never seems to consider our schedule or time constraints. The disciples had misguided expectations in the fourteenth chapter of Matthew. Jesus sent His band of twelve across the water to the other side while He dispersed a crowd of five thousand. Jesus had just fed them all with two fish and five loaves of bread. Certainly not enough to go around—but in His hands, anything is possible. We refer to it as "the miracle of the loaves and fishes." Focusing on Christ automatically brings multiplication and abundant supply. With the well-fed crowd gone and the disciples afloat, Jesus went up a mountain to pray.

INSTEAD OF REJOICING, THEY PANICKED

Meanwhile, the disciples faced a perilous storm. I'm sure they were praying, or at least frantically wondering, *Where is Jesus? Doesn't He know we're in trouble?* Matthew explains, "But the ship was now in the midst of the sea, tossed with waves: for the wind was contrary. And in the fourth watch of the night [somewhere between three and six AM], Jesus went unto them, walking on the sea" (Mt. 14:24–25). No doubt they were looking for another sailboat or, at least, someone rowing hard against the wind.

The eerie sight of a man walking on water drew this response: "they were frightened, saying, 'It is a ghost!' And they cried out for fear" (Mt. 14:26 NASB). With the answer to their prayer in full view, instead of rejoicing, they panicked. At times, truth is hard to recognize, especially when we try to predict how God will intervene to meet our needs. God often has a better idea.

A woman approached me one evening as I led a prayer line. She asked me to pray with her that God would give her an extra job. The Lord said, "Ask her why she wants to be tired all the time." I asked the question and she look puzzled. Then I asked her, "What do you really need—an extra job or a different job making more money?" I said I could agree with her for a new job with more income. We prayed together to that end. A week later she told me God opened the door for a job making more money than ever. God answered her prayer in a way she hadn't thought of. The new job not only gave her the extra needed income, it was easier on her physically. As usual, God had a better solution.

To illustrate the disciples' bewilderment at seeing an apparent mirage, I point you to an example from the Bible. A year or so after Pentecost, authorities arrested Simon Peter for preaching the Gospel. Luke, who wrote the book of Acts, tells us, "And when he [Herod] had apprehended him, he put him in prison, and delivered him to four quaternions of soldiers [sixteen total], to keep him; intending after Easter [Passover] to bring him forth to the people. Peter therefore was kept in prison: but prayer was made without ceasing of the church unto God for him" (Acts 12:4-5).

Bound with chains, Peter slept between two soldiers, and additional guards stood watch at the door. An angel woke Peter, told him to get dressed and follow him. Peter obeyed, not realizing it was really happening, "but thought he saw a vision" (Acts 12:9). Evidently, even Peter anticipated a much different solution to his problem. When will we learn? Isaiah gives a hint. "For my thoughts are not your thoughts, neither are your ways my ways, saith the Lord. For as the heavens are higher than the earth, so are my ways higher than your ways, and my thoughts than your thoughts" (Is. 55:8-9).

DON'T CHILDREN HAVE AN IMAGINATION THESE DAYS!

Meanwhile, some of the church folk were gathered at Mary's house to pray. This particular Mary was John's mother. Can you hear their prayer? "Oh, Lord. Please get our preacher out of jail!" Peter, now free, went to Mary's house and knocked on the door. A little girl named Rhoda heard the knock and asked who it was. Apparently, the saints were too busy praying to deal with visitors. "And when she recognized Peter's voice, because of her joy she did not open the gate, but ran in and announced that Peter was standing in front of the gate" (Acts 12:14, NASB).

Little Rhoda had no trouble believing it was actually Peter at the door. The grownups responded predictably. "And they said unto her, Thou art mad" (v. 15). Today they would say, "Don't children have an imagination these days!"

Children find it easy to believe in the miraculous, giving rise to the term, "childlike faith." Perhaps Jesus hinted at that when He said, "Except ye be converted, and become as little children, ye shall not enter into the kingdom of heaven" (Mt. 18:3).

Back at Mary's house, Rhoda kept insisting their pastor was knocking at the door, at which point the adults speculated, "It is his angel. But Peter continued knocking: and when they had opened the door, and saw him, they were astonished" (Acts 12:15-16). May the day hasten when answered prayer no longer astonishes us.

The disciples saw Christ walking on water and were startled. Peter's deliverance from jail astounded everyone except a child named Rhoda. God wants us to expect His help, in spite of the circumstances. The reality is, He always comes through. The sooner we can learn that simple truth, the sooner we will learn to rest in quiet confidence.

Years ago, I drove south in my old 1960 Chevy. Suddenly, the engine just quit and the car coasted to a stop. I had plenty of gas, so that wasn't the problem. I tried to restart it with no success, and quietly said, "Lord, I need your help." I was a young Christian in my twenties. Evidently, wisdom had not yet replaced faith, because I believed God would come to my rescue. Shortly, I decided to walk to the next exit and seek help. Little did I know, it was seven miles away.

When driving on an interstate highway, signs, trees, and barns fly by. When you are walking, you notice everything, including the irony of a solitary bug creeping up a speed limit sign. As I strolled along, I counted fence posts and admired colorful pebbles at the edge of the road. Walking that seven miles to the next exit took over an hour. A local garage mechanic wanted more than the last seven dollars in my pocket just to tow my vehicle.

Somewhat frustrated, I started back toward my car. After a mile or two, a benevolent driver picked me up and asked where I was headed. I explained my dilemma and he asked what kind of car I drove.

"Chevy," I said.

"V-8?" he asked.

When I replied, "Yes," he said he was a former Chevrolet mechanic and would be glad to help me. Now, God could have sent a Ford mechanic, but I wasn't driving a Ford, was I?

ODDS WERE AGAINST US

Shortly, we reached my disabled vehicle. He said, "Get in and turn it over." After a couple of revolutions, he said, "That's enough; it's your fuel pump." I explained I only had a pair of pliers and a screwdriver. "No problem," he said.

In a matter of minutes, he had the fuel pump off and we drove north to the nearest exit. It was Sunday *and* a holiday. Odds were against us. We found an open garage that just happened to have the fuel pump I needed. How much did it cost? You guessed it—seven dollars. Within thirty minutes, he installed the fuel pump and the car started right up. I begged him for his address so I could send him some money. He declined, saying, "Just remember to help somebody else when you get the chance."

I have tried to follow that good Samaritan's advice.

SKEPTICS CALL THAT LUCK OR COINCIDENCE

I had plenty of time to panic and many opportunities to doubt as I walked seven miles under a hot Florida sun. God knew something I didn't. That Chevy mechanic was driving toward me and God needed the hour it took me to walk the opposite direction so I would be going the right way when the mechanic drove by. Unbelievers call that luck or coincidence.

That reminds me of the skeptic who didn't believe in miracles. A preacher confronted him with the question, "What if you climbed to the top of a ten-story building, jumped off, landed on your head on the sidewalk below, and weren't even hurt. Wouldn't that be a miracle?"

The skeptic responded, "That would be an accident."

Not giving up, the preacher asked, "What if you did it all over again with the same result?

The skeptic quipped, "That, sir, would be a coincidence."

Persisting, the minister asked, "What if you jumped off the top of that building the third time and still weren't hurt?"

With a grin, the skeptic said, "Preacher, by that time, it would be a habit."

I mentioned my wife's car accident in chapter three. Here are a few more details. A pizza delivery driver rear-ended my wife as she waited to turn left onto our street. The resulting whiplash severely damaged two discs in her neck beyond repair. For three years, she endured constant headaches, limited neck movement, and no more than two or three hours sleep each night. In a constant state of discomfort and exhaustion, my dear wife accepted the ominous prospect of unrelenting pain and sleep deprivation for the rest of her life.

One day, after more than three years of misery from her injury, the phone rang. A friend and his wife were ministering in a local church and invited us to come. Judith and I went Sunday morning and enjoyed seeing old friends. We decided to go back Sunday night. After the message, our friend invited those with physical problems to come forward. He prayed for my wife and she was overcome by the power of the Holy Spirit. Moments later, she realized the soreness in her neck was gone. She could move her head and neck normally with no pain or restriction. From that day to this, she has been completely healed.

Why did God wait three and a half years? We have no idea. Judith just kept reminding God she would trust Him at all costs. One thing is certain: We should never give God a deadline when we ask for help. After nearly fifty years of following Jesus Christ, I am convinced He is trustworthy. Moreover, in His mind, He is never late. Could that be what Paul meant when he said, "Let this mind be in you, which was also in Christ Jesus?" (Phil. 2:5).

Never forget, even Jesus cried out, "My God, my God, why hast thou forsaken me?" (Mt. 27:46). He knows how we feel. He is truly "touched with the feelings of our infirmities" (Heb. 4:15). He gets it.

Chapter 7

WAITING IS A BUMMER

Lord, if You had been here, my brother would not have died (John 11:21 NASB)

I am not a good waiter. I hate waiting. Patience may be the best teacher, but why does it have to take so long? To make matters worse, God won't give us patience. He gives us wisdom, but not patience. James explains: "If any of you lacks wisdom, let him ask of God, who gives to all men generously and without reproach, and it will be given to him" (James 1:5 NASB). We get wisdom by asking. Patience doesn't come so easily.

In the preceding verses, James said, "My brethren, consider it all joy when you fall into divers temptations [trials]; Knowing this, that the trying of your faith worketh patience. But let patience have her perfect work, that ye may be perfect and *entire*, wanting nothing" (James 1:2-4, emphasis mine). The word "entire," according to Bullinger, means, "whole in every part, fixed in all its parts."

Patience is the last piece of the puzzle that makes a Christian whole. God never gets in a hurry, so impatient people may have a long wait before they experience His power. James said, "Let patience have her perfect work." The word "perfect" is from the Greek word *téleios*. It means, according to Bullinger, "what has reached its end term, or limit; hence complete, perfect, full, wanting nothing, *with special reference to the end for which it was intended."* Strong's Greek Dictionary adds, "*completeness:*—of full age."

We are talking about maturity, plain and simple.

GOD DOESN'T HAVE A DRIVE-THROUGH WINDOW

Impatience is common today. Everyone is in a hurry. We want instant potatoes, minute rice, ten-minute dinners, and thirty-minute oil changes. We expect everything to happen quickly, without any snags. We want what we want, when we want it, and we usually want it now. Unfortunately, God doesn't have a drive-through window. On a different seafaring occasion, the disciples accused Jesus of not caring when a storm threatened to sink them. Jesus, oblivious to the storm, slept soundly in the back of the boat. The disciples woke Him saying, "Teacher, do You not care that we are perishing?" (Mark 4:38 NASB).

In times of doubt, we should remember Jesus' words: "Are not two sparrows sold for a cent? And yet not one of them will fall to the ground apart from your Father. But the very hairs of your head are all numbered. Therefore do not fear; you are of more value than many sparrows" (Mt. 10:29–31 NASB). I can grasp the possibility that I'm worth more to God than a sparrow. It also comforts me to know He notices when a sparrow falls to the ground. It amazes me, however, that He has numbered every hair on my head. He doesn't just count the hairs and arrive at a total. He *numbers* them.

I remember my first year of college. I lived in a four-story dormitory with more than a hundred rooms. The dean had a key for each room on a huge keychain. I had heard he could feel any key with his eyes closed and tell what room number it fit. I challenged him one day to prove it. With his eyes closed, he invited me to choose some keys. He correctly guessed five keys in a row, just by feeling the edges. He made a believer out of me. I can see God going through the hairs of my head and putting a number on each one as His loving fingers gently touch hair after hair. What a mighty God we serve, and what a tender, caring Father He must be.

John, chapter 11, relates the story of Lazarus. A messenger told Christ his friend Lazarus was sick. Jesus already knew the circumstances through the Holy Spirit and said, "This sickness is not unto death, but for the glory of God, that the Son of God might be glorified thereby" (John 11:4). Jesus intentionally waited two more days before heading to Bethany. He knew Lazarus was dead and said so. "Then said Jesus unto them plainly, Lazarus is dead" (John 11:14).

It must have been a day's walk, because when they arrived, they learned Lazarus died four days earlier. It had taken a day for the messenger to reach Jesus. Jesus waited two more days, then made the daylong journey to reach Lazarus.

Martha immediately accused Jesus of waiting too long and said, "Lord, if You had been here, my brother would not have died" (John 11:21 NASB).

WE LOOK FOR TEMPORARY FIXES WHEN GOD WANTS LONG-TERM SOLUTIONS THAT TEACH ETERNAL LESSONS

Why did He wait so long? Our sense of fairness tempts us to question Jesus' thinking at times. Wouldn't it have been better if Jesus had healed Lazarus a few days earlier? As usual, we look for temporary fixes when God wants long-term solutions that teach eternal lessons. To her credit, Martha exhibited faith when she added, "But I know, that even now, whatsoever thou wilt ask of God, God will give it thee" (John 11:22).

Jesus replied, "Thy brother shall rise again" (John 11:23). Martha said, "I know that he shall rise again in the resurrection at the last day" (v. 24).

Her response gave rise to Jesus' classic statement, "I am the resurrection, and the life: he that believeth in me, though he were dead, yet shall he live: And whosoever liveth and believeth in me shall never die." (John 11:25-26).

These verses confused me as a youth. Christians do die, don't they? Of course they do, but I learned that Jesus was not talking about mere physical life, but resurrection life. Paul said, "If in this life only we have hope in Christ, we are of all men most miserable" (1 Cor. 15:19). Paul also said the time will come when "Death is swallowed up in victory (1 Cor. 15:54). We see death as a loss; God sees it as a victory. We see death as an end; God sees it as a beginning.

GOD SEES THE END WHILE WE ARE STILL STUCK IN THE TABLE OF CONTENTS

We live in a temporal world and have limited comprehension. God lives in eternity and sees the whole picture. "Remember the former things long past, For I am God, and there is no other; I am God and there is no one like Me, *Declaring the end from the beginning* And from ancient times things which have not been done, Saying, My purpose will be established, And I will accomplish all My good pleasure" (Is. 46:9-10 NASB, emphasis mine). God sees the end while we are still stuck in the table of contents. We see where we are—God sees where He wants to take us.

He knows who you will probably marry, what kind of ministry you will probably have, where you will probably live, and everything you will probably do. I use the word *probably* because we humans tend to come up with ideas and choices that are not part of God's plan. He hopes we all do everything He wants, but when we don't, God implements *plan B*.

Our goal is to discover and do His will. God hopes we discover and make *Him* our goal. His desire, I firmly believe, is to bring us into intimacy with Him. He has as many alternate plans as we have misdirected goals and poor choices. Until we come to know Him intimately, we will be limited in our ability to hear His voice and do His bidding. Intimacy cleans the wax out of our spiritual ears and opens the channel of communication. Lack of intimacy keeps us somewhat mystified about the Holy Spirit's workings. That may point to our real need for patience.

As we continue the story of Lazarus, Mary makes the same accusation as her sister, Martha: "Lord, if You had been here, my brother would not have died" (John 11:32 NASB). It suggests they were discussing Jesus' tardiness with a touch of criticism.

I love reading the Bible because, along with wonderful truth, it shows people making the same mistakes we do. I have been guilty of being angry with God, and, at times, upset with His lack of good timing. Furthermore, I really dislike it when I tell God about my great plans and I'm sure I can hear Him snickering in the background.

The miracle of Lazarus had greater implications than Mary or Martha or even the disciples realized. Jesus asked, "Where have ye laid him?" (John 11:34). They led Him to a grave with a huge stone blocking the opening.

When Jesus told them to move the stone, Martha protested, saying, "Lord, by this time there will be a stench, for he has been dead four days" (John 11:39 NASB). Circumstances often try to overrule faith.

Jesus responded to her reasoning and said, "Did I not say to you, if you believe, you will see the glory of God?" (John 11:40 NASB).

THEN JESUS GAVE A COMMAND
NO ONE COULD OBEY

Jesus then prayed a simple, thirty-seven word prayer, ending with the words "that they may believe that thou hast sent me" (John 11:42). The impending miracle would validate Christ as the Son of God and glorify the Father in the process. Then Jesus gave a command no one could obey. He told Lazarus to do the one thing he couldn't do. "He cried with a loud voice, Lazarus, come forth" (John 11:43). Anyone with common sense knew Lazarus could not come forth. He was dead. He had been dead four days. He was already decomposing. Yet, in spite of all the evidence to the contrary, "he that was dead came forth" (John 11:44).

Jesus had a habit of telling people to do the one thing they couldn't possibly do. In the city of Nain, Jesus stopped a funeral procession. A widow's only son had died. "And when the Lord saw her, he had compassion on her, and said unto her, Weep not. And he came and touched the bier [coffin]: and they that bare him stood still. And he said, Young man, I say unto thee, Arise. And he that was dead sat up, and began to speak. And he [Christ] delivered him to his mother" (Luke 7:13–15).

Another miracle occurred in Jerusalem at a spa-like setting called the Pool of Bethesda. Legend suggested an angel occasionally disturbed the water. The first infirmed person touching the rippling water would receive a miracle of healing. One man, lame for thirty-eight years, had all but lost hope. Jesus approached him and asked if he would like to be whole. Bystanders probably reacted with shock and dismay, and probably thought, "What kind of person asks a cruel question like that? He can't walk and everyone knows it."

Jesus ignored the impossibility of the situation and told the crippled man to do the one thing he couldn't possibly do.

He said, "Rise, take up thy bed and walk." John continues the narrative with the words, "And immediately the man was made whole, and took up his bed [mat] and walked: and on the same day was the Sabbath" (John 5:8-9). The man couldn't walk, but because Jesus told him to, he did.

IT DOESN'T COUNT—IT HAPPENED ON THE WRONG DAY

Religious bystanders reacted on cue. When they saw the healed man carrying his mat, they said, "It is the Sabbath day: it is not lawful for thee to carry thy bed" (John 5:10). They were saying in effect, "We don't care if you received a miracle. It doesn't count—it happened on the wrong day."

Jesus' ministry constantly flew in the face of religious intolerance. If you insist on following God fully, you will eventually find yourself faced with a choice. You can follow Christ, or conform to the traditional mindset that says, *this is the way we've always done it.*

Most tradition is fine. I love Sunday morning church services. I can't find stained glass anywhere in the Bible, but I love praying in an empty church with sunlight dancing through multicolored windows.

I enjoy studying the historical origins of what we do in the name of Christ. Martin Luther gave us the pulpit and the eleven AM Sunday service. Monks in the Middle Ages gave us candles and incense to solve the problem of dark, musty cathedrals. Sixteenth-century fashion gave us the backward white collar peculiar to ministers. Everyone wore the simple banded collars until the mid-1500s, when newer collar styles were introduced. All but the poorest-of-poor could afford the newer style. Preachers, along with other low-income people, became the sole wearers of the older style collars. It became a clerical trademark.

Patience alone leads to maturity and there are no shortcuts. Here in Florida, we enjoy fresh citrus fruit in season. The orange can teach us a thing or two about maturity. In the spring, the enticing scent of orange blossoms permeates the air and announces the birth of a new crop. By June, the trees are full of small, green oranges. Those oranges are not edible. They are dry and very bitter to the taste. They won't ripen until September or October. Nevertheless, those oranges are perfect—*for June.* All the praying and fasting in the world won't change June to October. By October, sweet, juicy, oranges dot the trees like Christmas ornaments.

You may not need a breakthrough; you may just need patience. Remember, you get wisdom by asking. Patience only comes through waiting. No treatment of patience is complete without referring to the classic verse about waiting. "But they that wait upon the Lord shall renew their strength; they shall mount up with wings as eagles; they shall run, and not be weary; and they shall walk, and not faint" (Is. 40:31). Interestingly, this verse is not really about waiting in the strictest sense. It has more to do with the wonderful results that come with waiting. The key word is "wait." Translated from the Hebrew word *kaw-vaw,* it means, according to Strong, "to bind together by twisting, to collect, to be gathered together, or to be joined."

Gesenius, in his Hebrew-Chaldee Lexicon, similarly says, "to twist, to bind (as a rope), to be strong, robust, and to expect, to await (perhaps from enduring)." It suggests waiting expectantly with the hope of being joined or intertwined with the Lord. David uses the same Hebrew word when he says, "*Wait* on the Lord: be of good courage, and he shall strengthen thine heart: wait, I say, on the Lord" (Ps. 27:14, emphasis mine).

I see believers as hundreds of small chords, methodically intertwined into a strong rope. The small strands become almost invisible as God patiently meshes us into His strength. We are still part of the overall picture, but the rope is the goal. It is truly amazing how a bunch of small strands of string, weak by themselves, can become a heavy rope able to hold a massive ship snuggly to a pier. I hear Paul admonishing us once more:

"That Christ may dwell in your hearts by faith; that ye, being rooted and grounded in love, May be able to comprehend *with all saints* what is the breadth, and length, and depth, and height; And to know the love of Christ, which passeth knowledge, that ye might be filled with all the fullness of God" (Eph. 3:17-19, emphasis mine).

Our spiritual comprehension grows in direct proportion to how well we accept our need for each other in God's family. One of the Holy Spirit's goals is helping us comprehend with all saints the big picture of who God is and what He intends. Paul gave us insight when he said, "For we know in part, and we prophesy in part" (1 Cor. 13:9). I know a part of God's plan and you know a part. If we share what we each know, we see a clearer vision of the purpose of God. I have a word from God and you have a word from God. If we combine what we each hear from God, our mutual understanding grows and our vision enlarges. Our mutual care for each other will allow us to see God in a new and different way. The more we see each other in the family of God as brothers and sisters the more we see God as our Father.

There is a potential problem, however. Most of us will wait patiently for others to share their part, because we feel our contribution is the icing on the cake. The reality is, the body of Christ can survive without you or me, especially if selfishness rules us. Paul warns, "For I say, through the grace given unto me, to every man that is among you, not to think of himself more highly than he ought to think" (Rom.

12:3). Paul cuts even deeper when he says, "Do nothing from selfishness or empty conceit, but with humility of mind let each of you regard one another as more important than himself; do not merely look out for your own personal interests, but also for the interests of others." (Phil. 2:3-4 NASB).

We are in this together and we desperately need each other. "Five of you will chase a hundred, and a hundred of you will chase ten thousand" (Lev. 26:7-8 NASB). Joshua 23:10 adds, "One man of you shall chase a thousand: for the Lord your God, he it is that fighteth for you, as he hath promised you."

When we focus on the One who fights for us, the enemy fears us no matter how small our numbers.

Chapter 8

DON'T GET AHEAD OF GOD

Wait, I say, on the Lord (Psalms 27:14)

I've heard it said, "You can't outrun God." I've also heard the warning, "Don't get ahead of God." Perhaps the best example of the latter is the story of Moses.

"And Moses was learned in all the wisdom of the Egyptians, and was mighty in words and in deeds" (Acts 7:22). He was highly educated and a great orator as well. "And when he was full forty years old, it came into his heart to visit his brethren the children of Israel" (v. 23). Be careful about what comes into your heart. Exodus 2:11 gives us a curious detail about his visit. Moses "spied an Egyptian smiting a Hebrew, one of his brethren. And he looked this way and that way, and when he saw that there was no man, he slew the Egyptian and hid him in the sand" (Ex. 2:11-12). Moses looked left, then right, and seeing no one watching, he acted. Sadly, Moses looked everywhere but up. Had he looked heavenward, God would have encouraged this impetuous deliverer of Israel to go back home and mind his own business until further notice.

Was Moses called by God to deliver Israel? Certainly, but not right away. How many times have we resisted the voice of the Holy Spirit and rushed to meet a need? The existence of a need does not give us an automatic green light. Timing is everything. When God asks us to do something, perhaps we should remember to ask Him *when* we should do it. It might be His will to act, but the time for action may be years in the future. If God calls you to be a missionary in Haiti, don't rush out and buy a new summer wardrobe. The clothes might not fit when the time comes.

Moses killed one Egyptian when God planned to drown thousands in the Red Sea forty years later. Joseph prematurely shared the vision of his eleven brothers bowing to him. God wanted the entire nation of Egypt to submit to him as Pharaoh's right-hand man, but not for years. Peter impulsively cut off a soldier's ear in the Garden of Gethsemane when God wanted him to fill thousands of ears with the truth of the resurrected Christ on the Day of Pentecost.

"Wait, I say, on the Lord" (Psalms 27:14).

As a result of Moses' impatience, he spent forty years in Midian, watching his father-in-law's sheep. Forty years of waiting because he got ahead of God. Yet it wasn't punishment. God knew Moses needed forty years to stop relying on himself and his own abilities. Remember, Moses was as highly educated as a man could be in that day, and an accomplished public speaker as well. He reeked of self-confidence and self-reliance. There's nothing wrong with being confident as long as it doesn't tempt us to think we have a better idea than God. Moses misunderstood the time factor. I've said for years, "Self-confidence is the feeling you have before you fully understand all the facts."

One day, after forty years of obscurity as a sheepherder, Moses saw a burning bush. Acts uses interesting terminology to describe the scene. "And *after forty years were expired,* there appeared to him in the wilderness of Mount Sina[i] an angel of the Lord in a flame of fire in a bush" (Acts 7:30, emphasis mine). Again, we see God's timing.

God spoke to Moses through the flame and said, "Put off thy shoes from thy feet: for the place where thou standest is holy ground" (Acts 7:33). Interestingly, "the bush burned with fire, and the bush was not consumed" (Ex. 3:2). There is a lesson in this unique bush. If God is in the bush, supernatural fire will be manifested, but the fire will not [cause] burnout. This is God's work, not ours. Paul agrees when he says, "For it is God who is at work in you, both to work and to will for His good pleasure" (Phil. 2:13 NASB). Jesus adds, "The Father that dwelleth in me, he doeth the works" (John 14:10). We should never confuse the bush with the fire of God nor should we ever become bush admirers.

PICK A BUSH, ANY BUSH

There was nothing special about the bush. *Any* bush would have qualified. God can even use a scraggly old bush like you or me. Pick a bush, any bush. It wasn't the bush— it was God in the bush that made all the difference.

Moses was intrigued: "He wondered at the sight" (Acts 7:31). While the world looks with wonder for its miracle man to solve global problems, the Church can rest in the faithfulness of the indwelling Christ. Isaiah 9:6 calls Him "Wonderful." Focusing on Christ fills us with wonder. He doesn't give us miracles; He is the miracle. He doesn't give us deliverance; He is our deliverance. He doesn't give us healing; He is our healing. Remember, He doesn't give us things—He gives us Himself.

We need Christ, period. *Who* He is must become more important than *what* He does. Moses focused on the burning bush, and almost missed God. If we aren't careful, we will focus on everything but Christ. The early church focused on nothing else. "And daily in the temple, and in every house, they ceased not to teach and preach Jesus Christ" (Acts 5:42). When was the last time you heard a sermon that focused on Christ and Christ alone?

A few thoughts about what the Bible calls the "spirit of antichrist" will help us understand the importance of the centrality of Christ. John used the phrase "spirit of the antichrist" when he warned believers about the antichristian philosophy that will prevail in the last days. He said, "Beloved, do not believe every spirit, but test the spirits to see whether they are from God; because many false prophets have gone out into the world. By this you know the Spirit of God: every spirit that confesses that Jesus Christ has come in the flesh is from God; and every spirit that does not confess Jesus is not from God; and this is the *spirit of the antichrist,* of which you have heard that it is coming, and now it is already in the world" (1 John 4:1–3 NASB, emphasis mine). I draw your attention to the term "antichrist," and in particular the prefix *anti.*

Preachers sometimes use Webster's Dictionary to define a Bible term. Often, the true meaning of the word is missed. To his credit, Webster does reveal the source of words from other languages. Many of our English words, for example, have their roots in the Greek language. The prefix "anti" is a good example. Webster defines "anti" as: "1: opposite in kind, position or action 2: opposing: hostile toward." Antibacterial soap is against germs. Antitrust laws shield us from business monopolies. Anti-American sentiment is against America's culture. We generally understand the prefix *anti* to mean "against."

The Greek, however, defines it differently. According to Strong, the word *anti* means "opposite to, i.e. instead of. Often used in composition to denote contrast, requital, substitution." The spirit of the antichrist is not just against Christ, but wants us to substitute something *instead of* Christ.

Satan doesn't care what we Christians focus on, as long as it is something, anything, other than Christ Himself. The myriad of denominational pet doctrines is a strong indication that the spirit of *instead of Christ* is alive and well in the Christian community. Some churches focus on baptismal formulas. Others focus on the Sabbath day, while others focus on how we dress. Again, I don't think Satan cares what we focus on as long as it isn't Christ.

Let's revisit the burning bush. Standing in the presence of God, Moses suddenly displays the attitude only time and experience can produce. God said, "I am the God of thy father, the God of Abraham, the God of Isaac, and the God of Jacob. *And Moses hid his face; for he was afraid to look upon God"* (Ex. 3:6, emphasis mine).

God doesn't want us to be afraid of Him, but He does want us to be in awe of Him. To fear Him, means to exhibit a reverence full of awe. He could destroy us, but because of His love, He won't. Moments later, God reminded Moses of his destiny, saying, "Come thou therefore, and I will send thee unto Pharaoh, that thou mayest bring forth my people the children of Israel out of Egypt" (Ex. 3:10). God's time had come. This is where the story really gets interesting.

Remember, "Moses was learned in all the wisdom of the Egyptians, and was mighty in words and deeds" (Acts 7:22). His response to God's intention to send him to Pharaoh is especially puzzling. "And Moses said unto God, Who am I, that I should go unto Pharaoh, and that I should bring forth the children of Israel out of Egypt?" (Ex. 3:11). Several times in chapter three, God assures Moses He will be with him.

Instead of embracing God's promise of support, Moses replies, "But, behold, they will not believe me, nor hearken unto my voice: for they will say, The Lord hath not appeared unto thee" (Ex. 4:1).

MOSES RESORTED TO SELF-DEGRADATION

For nine more verses, God promised Moses power to work various miracles to convince Pharaoh he is on a divine mission. Unconvinced, Moses resorted to self-degradation. He devalued himself saying, "Please, Lord, I have never been eloquent, neither recently nor in time past, nor since Thou hast spoken to Thy servant; for I am slow of speech and slow of tongue" (Ex. 4:10 NASB).

How could a man known to be a polished speaker say such things? Had he finally realized his talents and abilities were ineffective without the fire of God? One thing was certain—his fleshly confidence was gone.

Paul said, "For we are the true circumcision, who worship in the Spirit of God and glory in Christ Jesus and put no confidence in the flesh" (Phil. 3:3 NASB). What looked like punishment became Moses' salvation. He still had his education. He still knew how to speak effectively, but he no longer had confidence in his ability to accomplish spiritual tasks. He learned, without question, unless God is in your talent and activity, the spiritual benefit is always zero.

The gospel of Mark gives a clear example of our need to listen to God and not just run around meeting every need we find. In Mark's opening chapter, Jesus was going about the Father's business. He called Simon and his brother Andrew to follow Him. "And straightway they forsook their nets, and followed him" (Mark 1:18). Then Christ beckoned to James and his brother John, and they followed as well, leaving their father behind to mend the fishing nets alone. The call of Christ draws men in a powerful way.

The following Sabbath, Christ taught in the synagogue in Capernaum. While there, He healed a man with a demonic spirit. Amazed bystanders said, "What is this? A new teaching with authority! He commands even the unclean spirits, and they obey Him. And immediately the news about Him went out everywhere into all the surrounding district of Galilee" (Mark 1:27-28 NASB).

From the synagogue, Christ and His four new disciples went to the house of Simon and Andrew. Simon's mother lay sick with a fever. Jesus took her hand and the fever left. She promptly got up and cooked her guests a meal. As the sun sank low, Mark tells us, "And at even, when the sun did set, they brought unto him all that were diseased, and them that were possessed with devils. And all the city was gathered together at the door. And he healed many that were sick of divers diseases, and cast out many devils; and suffered not the devils to speak, because they knew him" (Mark 1:32-34). He didn't want the demonic spirits to speak because they knew He was the Messiah. It wasn't time yet for His Messianic aura to be unveiled to the world.

The next morning, Jesus rose very early and found a quiet, solitary place to pray. Simon and the others went looking and when they found him said, "All men seek for thee" (Mark 1:37).

HE DIDN'T EVEN GO BACK AND SAY GOODBYE

Do you get the picture? Jesus worked miracles one evening that attracted a whole town's attention. Next morning, a huge crowd gathered and Jesus was nowhere in sight. The disciples located Him and told Him of the opportunity back in town. Would you and I go back for such a marvelous chance to minister? No doubt. Were there needs to be met? Certainly. Did Jesus go back and minister? No, He did not. After the disciples told Him of the expectant crowd, Jesus said, "Let us go into the next towns, that I may preach there also: for therefore came I forth" (Mark 1:38). He didn't even go back and say goodbye.

Even Jesus knew not to depend on Himself. He said, "Truly, truly, I say to you, the Son can do nothing of Himself, unless it is something He sees the Father doing; for whatever the Father does, these things the Son also does in like manner" (John 5:19 NASB). Evidently, Jesus saw the Father leaving Capernaum and thought it best to follow Him. Maybe it is time we found out what God is doing and asked if we could follow along and do it with Him.

I wonder how many times I neglected to find out if God was involved in my spiritual venture before I pursued it. I wonder how many churches were started simply because someone said, "Hey, why don't we start a new church? There's a real need in that area."

Please don't misunderstand me. I'm not against new works, but there is a simple way to determine the true origin of a ministry. If God starts a work, nothing can stop it. If man starts a work, it will take every effort to keep it alive. In the words of the High Priest Gamaliel, concerning the ministry of Peter and the other apostles, "And now I say unto you, Refrain from these men, and let them alone: for if this counsel or this work be of men, it will come to nought: But if it be of God, ye cannot overthrow it; lest haply ye be found even to fight against God" (Acts 5:38-39).

Jesus should have the final word here. "I am the vine, you are the branches; he who abides in Me and I in him, he bears much fruit; for apart [severed] from Me you can do nothing" (John 15:5 NASB). Jesus fully depended on His Father and explained it in simple terms. "The Father that dwelleth in me, he doeth the works" (John 14:10).

He gave His Father all the credit. We can do no less.

WE CAN DO A LOT WITHOUT GOD'S HELP

Make no mistake, we can do a lot without God's help. We can make people laugh with humor. We can make people cry with a sad story. We can stir people up with spirited singing and we can even preach like we're under a heavy anointing.

Years ago, a friend preached a revival in a local church. One night the pastor asked, just before introducing him, "Would you like me to stir up the people for you?" With my friend's nod of approval, the pastor verbally created an emotional atmosphere in a matter of seconds. As the evangelist passed by to take the pulpit, the pastor whispered, "How was that?"

I have a close friend who worked in entertainment for many years before the Lord came into his life. On one occasion, He had as many as ten bands and lounge acts under contract. He also owned the bars where they performed. He remarked to me one day, "Ted, a few preachers remind me of some of the lounge acts I used to work with; it all seems rehearsed."

I visited my friend Arthur Leis in his home one year while he was on furlough from Africa. He shared something that made me think. He told me he couldn't wait to return to Africa, where the simple Gospel of Christ produced consistently miraculous results. He explained by telling me he just couldn't handle the "Hollywood gospel" he saw here in America. He wasn't suggesting the American gospel was ineffective. He was just uncomfortable with some of the methods.

The apostle Paul saw the same in his day and said so. "Some, to be sure, are preaching Christ even from envy and strife, but some also from good will; the latter do it out of love, knowing that I am appointed for the defense of the gospel; the former proclaim Christ out of selfish ambition rather than from pure motives, thinking to cause me distress in my imprisonment. What then? Only that in every way, whether in pretense, or in truth, Christ is proclaimed; and in this I rejoice, yes, and I will rejoice" (Phil. 1:15-18 NASB).

Another friend, a capable musician and worship leader, described his music ministry as a performance. May God help us avoid robotic performance when anointed ministry is what He provides for and desires. Holy Spirit, teach us the difference between fleshly activity and true spiritual work.

We all want to hear God's voice and Scripture teaches we can. "Faith cometh by hearing, and hearing by the word of God" (Rom. 10:17). The original language is more specific according to Marshall's Greek-English New Testament. "Then faith [is] from hearing, and the hearing through a word of Christ." *Rhema* is the root word in the Greek for a "word" of Christ. I agree with those who suggest the word, *rhema*, means the spoken word of Christ.

Jesus, as usual, should have the final word. "My sheep hear my voice, and I know them, and they follow me" (John 10:27). May we hear His voice and learn to follow before we try to lead. The safest place on earth is humbly walking with Christ wherever He leads.

Lord, forgive us for those times we act without asking You. May we always listen before we speak and prayerfully wait before we plunge ahead.

Chapter 9

CHEER UP

Be of good cheer; it is I; be not afraid.
(Matthew 14:27)

Moments after the disciples saw Him strolling on water during a violent storm, Jesus spoke words that have comforted believers for two millennia. He said, "Be of good cheer; it is I; be not afraid." As a young evangelist, I paraphrased that classic verse to say, "Cheer up; I am; don't worry about a thing." Among the many negative by-products of fear, loss of joy seems to be the most common, but 1 Thessalonians 5:16 teaches we can live in continuous joy. It says simply, "Rejoice evermore."

Nehemiah said, "The joy of the Lord is your strength" (Neh. 8:10).

David was more specific when he declared, "Thou wilt shew me the path of life: in thy presence is fulness of joy; at thy right hand there are pleasures for evermore" (Psalms 16:11). Joy is not a thing; joy is a person. David expressed that when he prayed, "O send out Thy light and Thy truth, let them lead me; Let them bring me to Thy holy hill, And to Thy dwelling places. Then I will go to the altar of God, To *God my exceeding joy*" (Psalms 43:3-4 NASB, emphasis mine).

The fact that Christ declared Himself to be the great I AM should be enough for any believer. When Moses asked why Israel should believe God sent him to lead them, the Lord replied, "Thus shalt thou say unto the children of Israel, I AM hath sent me unto you" (Ex. 3:14). Jesus made the same claim when Jewish leaders asked, "Whom do you make Yourself out to be?" (John 8:53 NASB).

Jesus said, "Your father Abraham rejoiced to see My day, and he saw it and was glad."

"The Jews therefore said unto Him, You are not yet fifty years old, and have You seen Abraham?" Jesus said to them, "Truly, truly, I say to you, before Abraham was born, I am" (John 8:56-58 NASB).

No one denies this is clearly a claim to deity. When He said, "I am," the Jews picked up stones to hurl at Him. They saw His claim as blasphemous. Christ's deity is the litmus test of Christianity.

JESUS—WHERE ARE YOU?

One of my favorite messages is titled "Jesus—Always on Time." It could just as easily be titled "Jesus, Where Are You?"

Experience has taught believers a stark reality. Jesus operates on a completely different schedule. He never comes when we think He should and He seldom answers prayer the way we expect. Look again at the context of the story in Matthew, chapter fourteen. In verse 22, Jesus told the disciples to get into a ship and cross to the other side while He sent the multitudes home. He then went up a mountain to pray. Then we notice the length of time involved: "And when the evening was come, He was there alone" (Mt. 14:23).

He prayed until late in the evening. Verse 24 tells us, "But the ship was now in the midst of the sea, tossed with waves: for the wind was contrary." It was probably stormy where Jesus was as well. The disciples must have fought the wind in that small ship for hours. "In the fourth watch of the night Jesus went unto them, walking on the sea" (v. 25). As I said earlier, the fourth watch was somewhere around four o'clock in the morning.

The miracle of Jesus walking on the water was not an instant happening. It developed over eight or ten hours. Jesus seems to have waited until the disciples had lost all hope of survival. We've all been there, haven't we?

That was certainly the case with Lazarus. Jesus waited until He knew Lazarus was dead and his sisters, Mary and Martha, had lost hope. Do you remember their frustration? "Lord, if thou hadst been here, my brother had not died" (John 11:21). Moments later, Jesus raised Lazarus from the dead. It was an instant miracle, but it was days in the making. Jesus intentionally waited until He knew Lazarus was dead. He preferred a resurrection over a healing.

Moses saw the sudden miracle of the burning bush, but that experience was forty years in the making. Poor Moses spent four decades watching his father-in-law's sheep. Joseph experienced an overnight promotion to the second-highest position in Egypt, answering only to Pharaoh himself. However, leading up to that promotion, he spent several years in prison for something he didn't even do.

The Bible is full of miracles, but we tend to overlook the span of time leading up to the miraculous events. Take time to reflect on the miracles you have seen in your own life. My wife, Judith, lived in constant pain for over three years before God instantly restored two crushed discs in her neck. Thank God for immediate, miraculous answers to prayer, but God often plows deep into our character before He unleashes His power. There are exceptions to that rule, but they are rare.

Never forget: God is more interested in developing our character than using us to work wonders.

WE WANT INSTANT FAITH AND INSTANT MIRACLES

I have already discussed patience, but some review will be helpful. God often wants something for us that requires our patience. We want instant faith and instant miracles. God wants the time He knows it will take to develop His Son's character in us. "But we all, with unveiled face beholding as in a mirror the glory of the Lord, are being transformed into the same image [of Christ] from glory to glory" (2 Cor. 3:18 NASB).

Our sinful tendencies will wane as the emerging character of Christ develops in us. The less we sin, the more the joy of the Lord will increase. As I said earlier, behavior doesn't build character. If God can teach us to trust Him, Christ's character will increasingly dominate our behavior. Our joy will thrive as Christ's character grows in us. Righteous behavior is the organic result of godly character.

Doing the right thing results in joy. Doing the wrong thing produces sadness. In Genesis, God accepted Abel's sacrifice and rejected Cain's. As a result, "Cain became very angry and his countenance fell" (Gen. 4:5). He got mad and stopped smiling. Righteous behavior brings joy and God told us so. The Lord said to Cain, "Why are you angry? And why has your countenance fallen? If you do well, will not your countenance be lifted up?" (Gen. 4:6-7 NASB). Just do the right thing—you will smile more.

It is finally now, in my autumn years, that I am beginning to understand our intense need to trust God's timing in all circumstances. As Paul put it, "I have learned, in whatsoever state I am, therewith to be content" (Phil. 4:11). May we truly come to the place where we no longer panic when trouble comes, but simply rest in quiet confidence as we patiently and cheerfully wait on the Lord to come to our aid. That confidence will attract the joy of the Lord like bees to flowers.

OUR CIRCUMSTANCES BECOME HIS CLASSROOM

I know, patient waiting is easier said than done. I believe God will use our difficult circumstances to teach us to trust Him. Because of our tendency to make poor choices, we have become experts at getting into trouble all by ourselves. On the other hand, things can happen that are out of our control. Either way, our circumstances become His classroom.

David said, "The Lord will perfect that which concerneth me" (Ps. 138:8). Peter lends to our understanding when he says, "And after you have suffered for a little while, the God of all grace, who called you to His eternal glory in Christ, will Himself perfect, confirm, strengthen and establish you" (1 Pet. 5:10 NASB). Peter makes no effort to identify the origin of our suffering. Remember, we are interested in getting results; God is interested in building our character. This is His deal, not ours. Power seldom precedes patience. If it does, the impatient one usually pays a price.

King Saul is a good example of the negative impact of impatience. He prophesied one day and tried to spear David the next. Power corrupted him because he lacked the patience God needed to build his character. Abraham and Sarah are another example of the negative consequences of impatience. In an effort to help fulfill God's promise of a son, she convinced her husband to sleep with her handmaid Hagar and she gave birth to Ishmael. His offspring became the Palestinian nation that has been a thorn in Israel's side for thirty-five hundred years. Today Ishmael's descendents threaten Israel's very existence. "Wait, I say, on the Lord" (Psalms 27:14). Be of good cheer while you wait.

Chapter 10

LORD, IS THAT REALLY YOU?

Lord, if it is You, command me . . .
(Matthew 14:28 NASB)

Picture the scene: The disciples finally realized Christ was not a mirage or a ghost as He walked on the water toward them. Peter, always quick to speak, shouts over the wind: "Lord, if that really is you, give me the okay to walk on the water."

Jesus said, "Come."

Finding courage to trust Christ for the impossible, Peter made his move. Was Peter being too bold? Not if Christ was on the scene and gave the word to proceed. No doubt, Peter's impulse to make such a request was prompted by the Lord. Too often our decisions are based on visible needs or our personal whims and we move without asking.

As I mentioned in chapter seven, Moses got ahead of God. He was anxious to move into his calling. If Moses had asked God before he went to "visit his brethren," God would have said, "No." Moses would have gone home and God would have found another way to plow deep into his character.

This is a perplexing question we all face. Is God in what I'm about to do? Is it okay to forge ahead and meet what looks like a real need? Now, if someone is drowning, it's not time to pray and ask God for permission to act. At the same time, if you can't swim, I don't recommend diving in to make the rescue. You should, however, figure out a way to help someone struggling to survive. Throw something toward them to keep them afloat. Flag down someone else who can swim. Call 911. Do something. It's not time to pray—it's time to act, and act quickly. I do believe God can prompt us to do what is necessary in emergencies. When it comes to doing God's will, however, timing is always a factor.

HE SAW ONE SCENE WHILE GOD SAW THE WHOLE PLAY

We tend to miss the big picture in favor of the immediate short story. Moses saw an opportunity that, by itself, seemed legitimate and honorable. He saw one scene, while God saw the whole play. Moses wanted to help his fellow Israelites and God agreed with that plan. God put the desire in Moses' heart to begin with. The plan was right—the timing was all wrong. If God puts something in your heart, He will bring it to pass in His own good time.

God is a scheduler. We can't hurry or change God's perfect timing. Scripture is replete with God's habit of following a preconceived schedule. "And when the Day of Pentecost was fully come . . . suddenly there came a sound from heaven" (Acts 2:1, 2). "When the fulness of the time was come, God sent forth His son" (Gal. 4:4).

God wanted Moses to lead Israel out of Egypt, but not for forty years. There was nothing magic in that time span. God had several things in view. First He needed a proud, strong-willed Pharaoh in place. At the same time, God needed forty years to soften a proud, headstrong Moses. Moses wanted a revolution in Israel, but God wanted a revolution in Moses' heart. The poor man probably spent years blaming himself for something God would have arranged either way. Those forty years were more necessary than Moses could ever have imagined.

AT THE END OF THE DAY, GOD GETS HIS WAY

Yes, we can muck up the waters if we move prematurely, but God then moves to plan B and accomplishes His desires another way. At the end of the day, God gets His way. We may suffer a little more if we resist God's direction, but we will suffer nonetheless. If Jesus learned obedience by the things He suffered, we should be willing to follow His example. Our suffering often means God is working His will in our lives. He doesn't cause the suffering, but He can use it for our benefit and His glory.

I know there are some who insist we should not have to suffer and God never uses suffering to teach us anything. Peter seems to disagree: "Beloved, think it not strange concerning the fiery trial which is to try you, as though some strange thing happened unto you: But rejoice, inasmuch as ye are partakers of Christ's sufferings; that, when his glory shall be revealed, ye may be glad also with exceeding joy" (1 Pet. 4:12-13). God may not arrange fiery trials, but He will certainly utilize them to refine our hearts and purify our motives.

God allowed Satan to attack Job, then used it to set Job free from self-centered thinking. We see the circumstances in our present situation, while God sees the end result. He wants to free us from the bondage of self-rule.

When can we expect to see the miraculous begin to flow in our lives? Something I've noticed in my own life might be helpful. On reflection, I remember God's miraculous intervention from time to time through my entire Christian experience. Our problem seems to be our need for much ado and excitement when God does something miraculous. We forget—He doesn't need the drama. When God does something supernatural, it is miraculous to us, but natural for Him. He acts supernaturally and we say, "Wow!"

More often than not, God moves supernaturally and we see the results in the normal, everyday world. As a result, God often answers our prayer in a quiet, simple way with little or no fanfare. God had me pray for a man with bad knees with no noticeable result. Six months later he told me three days had passed before he realized his knees were no longer bothering him. Perhaps we should just live and move in God's natural environment and expect miracles as a matter of course.

Peter, on the other hand, was rash and impulsive. He heard Jesus say, "Come," and he acted without thinking. He skipped baby steps and took a giant leap. Here is an interesting question: Could Peter walk on the water and hold onto the main mast at the same time? Are we guilty of asking God for a miracle while we stay on the safe side of risk? This is not rocket science. Before Peter had a chance to participate in a miracle, he had to be willing to do something that risked everything. I'm not there yet and you probably aren't either, but, looking back, I see God's hand leading me to take baby steps into believing for miracles. You might see His hand in your past as well if you look.

IT WAS A "LORD, IS THAT YOU?" MOMENT

As a young evangelist, I remember God's gentle promptings to take a risk. As I finished preaching in a local church one evening, God began to speak to me about a woman sitting over on my right. She was praying fervently as I gave an altar call for the sick. The Lord spoke to me and said, "That lady is praying and saying, 'Lord, if you are in that little preacher, have him call me out and tell me I have sugar diabetes, and I believe you will heal me.'"

It was a *LORD, is that you?* moment. I had been hearing things like that occasionally, but thus far had not acted. I took a risk and told her what I thought I heard from the Lord. She excitedly verified I was hearing from God and He richly blessed her and others who heard our conversation.

Baby steps can soon lead to big steps. I got out of my comfort zone and Jesus met me on the water. He won't push us out of the boat. He is a gentle and loving Master who will gently nudge us into participating with Him in His supernatural workings.

If we purpose in our hearts to trust God and commit to follow Him fully, the time will come when we begin to see His hand revealed in increasingly supernatural ways.

Just a word of caution. If you start looking for opportunities to work miracles, you may be putting the cart in front of the horse. Remember, God is a scheduler. Don't get ahead of Him. It's not worth it. The time may come when you have to run to keep up with Him. For now, learn to wait and you will seldom be disappointed. In time, you will learn to recognize His voice and follow His lead.

Chapter 11

BE PREPARED FOR MISHAPS

Lord, save me. (Matthew 14:30)

Peter actually walked on the water—*for a few seconds.* "But when he saw the wind boisterous [tempestuous], he was afraid; and beginning to sink, he cried, saying, Lord, save me."

Countless sermons have dealt with the *if only* factor in this familiar story. If only he had kept his eyes on Jesus; if only he had ignored the wind and the waves; if only.... If he only took two steps on the water before he began to sink, it was still an indescribable event. I would have spent the next few months (if not years) reminding myself of the two-step miracle. Two steps are better than none. Add to that the fact that he had the courage to try and you have an unforgettable experience.

Eventually we must decide to try, especially if the Lord Himself is urging us on. How can we know if it's really Him? We won't know until we try.

A speaker at a motivational seminar said something I will never forget. He said, "Most people tiptoe through life in order to make it safely to death." I'm not challenging anyone to do something dangerous or foolish, but let's face it: anything we do for the Lord will appear silly or even perilous to the unbelieving mind.

IN THAT WILD MOMENT PETER FOCUSED ON CHRIST

What was Peter thinking when he asked the Lord for permission to walk on the water? What was running though his mind when he let go the main mast and stepped out of the boat onto an uncertain surface? The unrelenting storm had probably chilled him to the bone. The wind was still whistling and the waves continued to crash against the little vessel as he dared to take that first fateful step. Talk about distractions! Still, he had the courage to try.

Somehow, he knew Christ would be the reason he could walk on water. You and I must learn the same lesson. In that wild moment, Peter focused on Christ and that led to a miraculous experience, only interrupted when he took his eyes off Jesus to look at the storm. The wind and waves, for a moment, took precedence over the presence of Christ Himself. Faith giving way to fear, Peter began to sink and cried, "Lord, save me."

"Immediately Jesus stretched out His hand and took hold of him" (Mt. 14:31 NASB). The important thing to remember is this: Peter knew what to do as he began to sink. He cried out to the Lord for help. Did he believe he could continue walking on the water after a momentary glitch in faith? Verse 32 continues, "And when they got into the boat, the wind ceased" (NASB).

What happened between the moment Jesus caught His sinking disciple and the time it took to get back to the boat? I have no problem seeing the two of them walking back to the boat *on the water*. With his faith restored, Peter regained his footing, but this time Christ walked beside him. What a scene that must have been. With all our faith teaching, our deeper-life conferences, and our appetite for fresh revelation, there is still nothing more powerful than walking hand in hand with Jesus. If we lose our footing, He simply tightens

His grip. David saw the picture centuries earlier and wrote, "The steps of a man are established by the Lord; and He delights in his way. When he falls, he shall not be hurled headlong; Because the Lord is the One who holds his hand" (Ps. 37:23-24 NASB).

Teach us, Holy Spirit, to keep a firm grip on the Master's hand, even after the storm passes.

Chapter 12

STORMS ARE TEMPORARY

The wind ceased. (Matthew 14:32)

Christ challenged Peter to walk on water and the impetuous disciple dared to obey. The result was a miracle to behold. A moment of doubt interrupted the supernatural event, but Christ intervened the very second Peter called for help. He wanted His disciple to finish what he started in spite of his doubt. They arrived back at the boat and, without a word from anyone, the wind ceased. The presence of Christ restores normalcy.

Psalms 23:3 comes to mind. David said, "He restoreth my soul." The word "restoreth," according to Strong's Concordance, means "to turn back." The explanation goes on to suggest, not turning back to the starting point, but "to recover," or "refresh," "to draw back," or "to fetch home again." Peter recovered when the firm grip of Christ restored his confidence. He simply took up where he left off. When Jesus took his hand, Peter regained his footing on the stormy sea and they walked back to the boat together.

I know the Bible doesn't specifically say all that, but I'm convinced it happened that way. Perhaps Peter recalled the words of Christ, spoken only minutes earlier. "Cheer up; I am; don't worry about a thing."

I have doubted Christ many times over the years, only to watch Him show up with the answer to my plight. Each time He comes through, I promise myself I will never doubt Him again, only to break that promise the moment a new trial presents itself. Without fail, Christ consistently proves He is equal to the task and master of our circumstances. His presence always stills the storm and calm prevails. Our doubt may disappoint Him, but He never forsakes us or turns away. Our alleged insurmountable circumstances only spur Him on.

If He has to walk on a stormy sea to get to us, He will. He walked through flames to protect three Hebrew boys in a fiery furnace (Dan. 3:23-25). He proved to Daniel, lions are not worth a moment's worry (Dan. 6:12-21). He showed the nation of Israel, no obstacle can stop His children's progress, not even an impassable sea (Ex. 5:14-22). What looked like a dead end became a door to the promise land.

There is not enough room in this book to recount the timeless stories in the Bible of God's divine intervention in His children's lives. I take comfort in the Children of Israel. They never seemed to learn. Sometimes I wonder if I will ever stop panicking when trouble comes. Peter is helpful here. "Grace unto you, and peace, be multiplied" (1 Pet. 1:2). God multiplies and piles up grace and peace because He knows we will always need more. Lest we forget, the Lord said, "My strength is made perfect in [your] weakness" (2 Cor. 12:9). It's never about *our weakness*—it's always about *His strength*.

I never want to get to the place I don't need His help. Christ is very specific about our need to trust Him fully. There are many things we can do without God's help. Godless people have proven that for thousands of years.

The people who built the tower of Babel are an example of what men can do when they put their minds to it. The book of Genesis tells us, "And they said, 'Come, let us build for ourselves a city, and a tower whose top will reach into heaven, and let us make for ourselves a name'" (Gen. 11:4 NASB). God noticed their determination and said, "Behold, they are one people, and they all have the same language. And this is what they began to do, and now nothing which they purpose to do will be impossible for them" (Gen. 11:6, NASB).

Unity is powerful. May Jesus' prayer to the Father become a reality in the Church. "And the glory which Thou hast given Me I have given to them; that they may be one, just as We are one; I in them and Thou in Me, that they may be perfected in unity, that the world may know that Thou didst send Me" (John 17:22-23 NASB). The world will notice a unified church because Christ can be comfortable there.

PAUL GAVE US A LESSON IN CONSTRUCTION

To help us understand the difference between fleshly effort and true spiritual activity, Paul gave us a lesson in construction. "For no man can lay a foundation other than the one which is laid, which is Jesus Christ. Now if any man builds upon the foundation with gold, silver, precious stones, wood, hay, straw, each man's work will become evident; for the day will show it, because it is to be revealed with fire; and the fire itself will test the quality of each man's work" (1 Cor. 3:11-13 NASB).

The analogy is simple. Fire refines and purifies gold and silver. Precious gems can withstand the intense heat and pressure required to form them. Wood, hay, and stubble, on the other hand, go up in a wisp of smoke. If Christ is not the foundation, our work becomes dust and ashes. With Christ as our foundation, we can echo with Daniel, "The people that do *know* their God shall be strong, and do exploits" (Dan. 11:32, emphasis mine).

Daniel uses the Hebrew word "yada" for *know*. When the Bible says, "And Adam knew Eve his wife; and she conceived, and bare Cain" (Gen. 4:1), the word, *yada,* is the root word for "knew." Again, we are talking about true intimacy in relationship. Those who know God in a true and intimate way will do mighty things in the name of Christ.

WE SHOULD RUN FROM THE SPOTLIGHT AS FAST AS WE CAN

I see a simple test to prove the validity of what we do for Christ. If we can take credit, then we most likely did it all by ourselves. If Christ did it through us, we should run from the spotlight as fast as we can. It is entirely possible to be in the precarious position of competing with God for credit—a competition we will surely lose. It makes me very uneasy when I hear a pastor talking about the great church he built or the great work that grew up under his leadership. I'm uncomfortable talking about *my* ministry. It's *His* Church and *His* ministry.

I heard James Robison speak at a local Bible college several years ago. He shared the time that God spoke to him and said, "James, I've seen your ministry for several years now—how would you like to see mine?"

We are instrumental, of course, when God does something. That means simply, we are His instrument. A master brick mason can build a beautiful structure. Should the trowel he used take any credit? Hardly. Without the master mason's skill, a trowel is an idle tool.

Having a bit of experience laying concrete block and brick, I have a well-worn trowel. It is somewhere in my garage. It has one purpose these days: I use it to remove the charcoal ashes from our barbeque grill. It builds nothing; it does nothing really important other than ash removal. I could still pick up that old trowel and build something beautiful. I just don't choose to use it that way anymore. I do use it at times to dig up weeds in my yard—a lowly job for such a tool.

Is that analogy too close to home? I don't want to think about past foolish decisions when I dared take credit for something God did. He will put you or me on a shelf if we dare touch His glory. I've been on that shelf. It's lonely up there. I would much rather be used to build something for eternity. I just need to remember who really deserves the credit. It's not about me—I'm just the trowel.

THE REAL WORK OF GOD IS BELIEVING

Jesus said something extraordinary when someone asked Him one day, "What shall we do, that we may work the works of God?"

"Jesus answered and said to them, 'This is the work of God, that you believe in Him whom He has sent'" (John 6:28-29 NASB).

Apparently, believing is the real work of God. Faith is not a physical act. The Levite priests in the Old Testament could not wear certain things when they ministered to the Lord in the sanctuary. "Linen turbans shall be on their heads, and linen undergarments shall be on their loins; they shall not gird themselves with *anything which makes them* sweat" (Ez. 44:18 NASB). The meaning is obvious. True ministry to the Lord should cause no sweat. If you sweat a lot in the ministry, you might want to rethink your methods. How much is you and how much is Him?

I'm reminded of a story I heard years ago. A pastor of a large church had a daily habit of driving to the outskirts of the town he lived in and sitting on a hillside. Out of curiosity, someone followed him one day and asked him why he did it. Pointing across the valley, the pastor said, "Every day about this time that train comes through town. It's the only thing that moves around here without me having to push it."

The writer of Hebrews puts the icing on the cake when he reminds us, "For we who have believed enter that rest"

(Hebrews 4:3 NASB). He concludes by saying, "There remains therefore a Sabbath rest for the people of God. For the one who has entered His rest, has himself also rested from his own works, as God did from His" (Heb. 4:9-10 NASB).

The word "rest" is from the Greek word *sabbata,* meaning "Sabbath." However, the Holy Spirit is suggesting something more than just a day of rest. He is talking about resting in Christ—not just one day a week, but every day.

I hear you protesting. "Ted, if I do that, nothing will happen." I would ask, "What is happening now that is out of the ordinary?" We should remember our place in God's family. God has "raised us up together, and made us sit together in heavenly places in Christ Jesus" (Eph. 2:6).

Notice, He *made* us sit. Our position in Christ is sitting with Him. We work from a sitting position. We fight from a sitting position. May we learn to minister from a sitting position. In other words, we live and act in a state of rest. Paul adds to our discussion when he says, "Fight the good fight of faith" (1 Tim. 6:12). He further reminds us, "For though we walk in the flesh, we do not war after the flesh: (For the weapons of our warfare are not carnal [fleshly], but mighty through God to the pulling down of strongholds)" (2 Cor. 10:3-4).

FAITH IS A SWEAT-FREE ENDEAVOR

Our fight, our wrestling, our struggle is not fleshly, but spiritual and, as such, is a fight of faith. If our fight was physical, there would be sweat indeed, but faith is a sweat-free endeavor. Picture the little boy whose father insisted he sit down at the dinner table. The lad wanted to eat standing up. Reluctantly, he sat down but insisted, "I may be sitting down on the outside, but on the inside I'm still standing up."

We can stand against the Satan's wiles while we sit with Christ in the heavenlies. Nestle in Christ as you wrestle. Don't struggle against the enemy. Snuggle with Christ as you shout with David, "You come to me with a sword, a spear, and a javelin, but I come to you in the name of the Lord of hosts, the God of the armies of Israel, whom you have taunted" (1 Sam. 17:45 NASB).

We face giants today that are bigger than any David ever fought. The evil that seems to prevail around the globe is like nothing we have ever seen. It is as daunting to us as Goliath was to David. On the other hand, the power and glory that God is going to express through His followers in these last days will be like nothing Satan has ever seen. Just as surely as Goliath fell, Satan and his rebel forces are going down.

David knew the secret to a sweat-free life of faith and made that very clear when he faced Goliath. Seemingly without fear, he shouted in the giant's face, "And all this assembly shall know that the Lord saveth not with sword and spear: for the battle is the Lord's, and he will give you into our hands" (1 Sam. 17:47). Notice, he didn't say *my* hands. He said *our* hands. As a youth, he already knew he couldn't do anything alone. He was ready to credit his fellow warriors with the imminent victory.

His fearlessness surfaced when he asked a few verses earlier, "What shall be done to the man that killeth this Philistine, and taketh away the reproach from Israel? for who is this uncircumcised Philistine, that he should defy the armies of the living God?" (1 Sam. 17:26). David knew victory was certain if he fought God's way. His only question was, "What do I get?" His reward, he learned, would be great riches, the king's daughter for a wife, and exemption from taxes for his entire family. Knowing David, the riches and the king's daughter were incidental benefits. I have no doubt his first desire was to bless his father and family with permanent relief from taxes.

David had inside information. He knew if Goliath defied Israel, he defied God Himself. The giant was a dead man walking and didn't even know it. David sensed it was only a matter of time. He looked past the towering warrior and saw the victorious aftermath—an unconscious giant, flat on his back. Satan and all the Goliaths he can muster cannot overcome a believer who fully trusts the invincible God.

WHO DOES THE DEVIL THINK HE IS?

I often wonder why Satan continues to fight against the people of God, knowing destruction is his destiny. He can't defeat us and he knows it. Satan may win temporary skirmishes, but in the end, we will be victorious. The devil's pride is his downfall. Pride will drive you to fight, even when you are dead wrong. Goliath was ignorant of one thing David knew to be true: "This day will the LORD deliver you up into my hands, and I will strike you down, and remove your head from you. . . that all the earth may know that there is a God in Israel" (1 Sam. 17:46, NASB). Moments earlier in verse 26, David asked, "Who is this uncircumcised Philistine, that he should defy the armies of the living God?" We should be asking the same question today—*Who in the world does the devil think he is?*

Satan has not forgotten what a boy did to Goliath. I suspect he has the same uneasiness when he ponders what God's people might do to his rebel kingdom if they join hands and start focusing on Christ and Christ alone. Seas could part, walls could collapse, and giants could fall.

Let's revisit God's armor in Ephesians, chapter six. It appears we must stand at times and temporarily suspend sitting. "Stand therefore, having your loins girt about with truth, and having on the breastplate of righteousness" (v. 14). Truth is the underlying reality of what seems to be. It looked like Peter was going to sink, but Jesus overruled the circumstances. Righteousness to me is not just right standing with God. Righteousness is that which conforms to the revealed will of God. Doing God's will is simply doing what He wants, and doing it His way and not ours.

If Christ wants us to walk on water, then we will walk on water. The circumstances are irrelevant.

The indwelling presence of Christ inspires us to be ready at all times to face our Goliaths. "Above all, taking the shield of faith, wherewith ye shall be able to quench all the fiery darts of the wicked" (v. 16). In order for the shield of faith to protect us, we must face the enemy and never turn away.

Faith, remember, is total trust in and obedience to Christ. Trust and obey, and the flaming missiles of the enemy will be extinguished time after time. We may get discouraged and possibly grow weary, but the shield of faith will protect us and keep us charging forward. "And take the helmet of Salvation, and sword of the Spirit, which is the word of God" (v. 17). Salvation means deliverance. The helmet of salvation protects our heart and mind and delivers us from the evil one.

Satan's fiery darts are almost always mental. He lies, lies, lies. *You're going to sink. You're going to lose. You're going to fail.* All lies. God's word tells us just the opposite. We will not sink, lose, or fail—not in the overall scheme of God. Christ is our foundation in sinking sand, our victory in temporary losses and our restorer after temporary failure. David said, "The battle is the Lord's" (1 Sam. 17:47). The battle is always His. The victory is always ours.

COWBOYS AND INDIANS

What should we do when we fail? One of my favorite verses is Micah 7:8, "Rejoice not against me, O mine enemy: when I fall, I shall arise; when I sit in darkness, the Lord shall be a light unto me."

When I was a boy, my friends and I played cowboys and Indians. We never had enough Indians. We often ran short of cowboys as well. We devised a simple solution. If you got shot, or took an arrow, you fell down, counted to ten and got right back up, good as new. I wonder if Micah had something like that in mind. Paul certainly understood the concept when he wrote, "We are troubled on every side, yet not distressed; we are perplexed, but not in despair; Persecuted, but not forsaken; cast down, but not destroyed" (2 Cor. 4:8-9). It's not a sin to be troubled, perplexed, attacked, or toppled.

Today, if I fall, I don't count to ten. I just whisper a prayer for forgiveness and get right back up. The alternative, just lying there in misery and defeat, is not the answer. Stop pouting, grieving and fretting. Get up! As Yogi Berra said, "It ain't over till it's over," and, I promise you, it is far from over.

Paul sums up, saying, "Always bearing about in the body the dying of the Lord Jesus, that the life also of Jesus might be made manifest in our body" (2 Cor. 4:10). We have a unique life in us. It is resurrection life. Resurrection life is only possible after death. Need I remind you? The cross Jesus commands us to pick up and carry daily has only one purpose—crucifixion. The cross is surely going to kill us. Those who seek to live the Christian life without mishaps will be sorely disappointed. There will be a thousand little crucifixions and, from time to time, a few major cross experiences.

I have said for years that those who want to serve God fully will experience at least a small taste of what Christ felt when He cried out, "My God, my God, why hast thou forsaken me?" (Mark 15:34). What a foolish but necessary prayer we all prayed when we were young Christians. "Lord, whatever it takes for You to use me, let it be." Do you remember that prayer? Who knew it would mean inevitable crucifixion? We cannot lay down that cross, for resurrection life comes after crucifixion.

The more traumatic the crucifixion experience, the greater the resulting life. Your failures are not a concern to God. The blood of His Son covers your sins and gives Him amnesia.

When the cross is working in your life, it doesn't mean He has forsaken you—it means He wants to use you without limits. Furthermore, when the cross has done its work, God won't have to worry about your ego getting in His way.

Chapter 13

IT'S ALL ABOUT WHO YOU KNOW

Thou art the Son of God. (Matthew 14:33)

The common phrase, "It's not what you know, but who you know," is especially true in the Christian life. I lived many years as a Christian before I began to realize God wanted me to know Him intimately. We use phrases in Christianity we don't always understand. We ask, "Do you have a relationship with Jesus?" We see that relationship as having our sins forgiven. As a result, we go to heaven instead of hell. It took me years to realize knowing Christ is much, much more than just forgiveness.

As a young evangelist, I preached a revival in a Florida church. The pastor and his wife kept talking about really knowing Jesus. They used the phrase "coming alive in Christ," and referred to it as the "Christ life." During that two-week period, the Holy Spirit began to intrigue me with the possibility of really knowing the Lord in an intimate way.

Up to that point, I had worshipped an external God. He always seemed to be somewhere besides right here. Occasionally, usually during a church service, God would manifest His power, and I went home with a strong sense of His nearness. Soon, however, His presence would slowly fade, making Him seem distant once again. I assumed that was the way He wanted it.

My Christian life became a chore of always trying to sense his presence, usually with limited success. I finally discovered, to my dismay, I knew Him savingly but I did not know Him intimately. I knew I would go to heaven if I died, but the Lord seemed generally aloof and often inaccessible to me. I felt undeserving of anything more. Thankfully, over time, the Lord taught me it's not *what* I know about Him, but how *well* I know Him personally that matters.

Can I really know Him intimately? Can I dare believe He loves me even more than a good earthly father loves his children? Does He really want to visit and fellowship with me daily as He did Adam and Eve? Occasionally, I think about my own father. After college, I decided I wanted to start hunting. I remembered he had a shotgun. Thinking he would probably give me his gun, I went to visit him and my mother. He told me he sold the gun years ago. It occurred to me I was a bit thoughtless. I went to see my father just to get something from him. I wondered how often I'd gone to my heavenly Father for purely selfish reasons.

I could always tell when my own children wanted something when they were young. They each had a way of being extra nice. Not that my kids weren't always nice to me, generally, but wanting something made them act a little differently, a little nicer for the moment. I began to feel shame for the times I had gone to my heavenly Father just to get something, instead of just prayerfully entering His presence to fellowship.

Slowly, over the years, the Holy Spirit has moved my attitude from self-centered to God-centered thinking. Now, as I practice thinking about Him instead of focusing on myself, my attitude prospers and my confidence in Him solidifies. Today I am convinced I have all the faith I need. I hope I can convince you of the same.

Peter kept reminding us of spiritual basics. "Wherefore I will not be negligent to put you always in remembrance of these things, though ye know them, and be established in the present truth" (2 Pet. 1:12). The "things" he refers to are faith, virtue, knowledge, temperance, patience, godliness, brotherly kindness, and charity. He concludes this basic list of essentials by saying, "But he that lacketh these things is blind, and cannot see afar off, and hath forgotten that he was purged from his old sins" (2 Pet. 1:5-9).

DON'T FORGET THE BASICS

I've always enjoyed watching the Davis Cup tennis competition. Various countries around the world send teams to compete for world title status in tennis. During a crucial singles match between America and a rival country, a spectator overheard advice the American coach gave his player. Hoping to learn some magical secrets he had never heard before, the spectator, who related the story, leaned closer to hear. He was startled to hear the coach, a former tennis star himself, rattle off the most basic advice.

"Remember to bend your knees, follow through. Don't rush your shots and be patient."

The spectator realized the lesson: *Don't forget the basics.* If you forsake the basics of the Christian walk, your growth will be stunted and your spiritual strength limited.

We have a tendency, as we grow in our faith, to forget the elementary steps that brought us into the kingdom. We forget to be as trusting as little children. Paul agrees when he says, "As you therefore have received Christ Jesus the Lord, so walk in Him" (Col. 2:6 NASB). How did you receive Christ? Did you tell Him how lucky He was to have you as His disciple? Did you suggest He made a wise choice when He saved you?

Did you not, in fact, come to him with brokenness and humility, begging His mercy and forgiveness? Weren't you grateful that He did not give you the judgment you really deserved? Have you forgotten to walk with that same humility and contriteness?

Wisdom comes with maturity, but it must never replace simple, childlike faith. Peter may have acted with childish impulsiveness when he made his remarkable request to walk on water, but Jesus honored his boldness. Peter's faith was sporadic, but he learned a crucial truth of the Gospel: With Christ, nothing is impossible.

In due time, this impulsive disciple became a fearless apostle and pioneer of the early church. He came to know the Lord in a true and intimate way.

Perhaps our most important need is learning to know the Lord intimately. If you still struggle with the possibility that you don't yet know Christ as intimately as you are destined to, take a step back and look at your life. Do you want to hear His voice more clearly and more often? Do you wish you were more aware of your purpose in His kingdom? Can you see your need to be more in tune with the Holy Spirit as He fulfills the will of the Father and Son on earth? Can you dare believe He wants to use you in ways you have only dreamed of until now? Are you concerned with what seems to be a real lack of the miraculous in the Body of Christ today?

Are you willing to commit yourself, not to pursuit of the miraculous, but to the time the Holy Spirit needs to build the character of Christ into you? Can you be content with knowing Him and knowing Him well above all else?

I JUST WANT TO KNOW THE LORD

As a teenage Christian, I became intrigued with the gifts of the Spirit, prophecy, miracles, and all the fascinating things that embodied the supernatural work of the Holy Spirit on earth. I longed to be used by Christ in every area of ministry and service. I spent years experiencing momentary joy in small victories, followed by recurring frustration and a far too frequent inability to do His will. I constantly failed to live what I thought should be a perfect life.

Decades later, I am still intrigued with spiritual things, but my focus is completely different. Today, I just want to know the Lord.

One of my favorite verses is often misquoted. Paul said, "I know whom I have believed, and am persuaded that he is able to keep that which I have committed unto him against that day" (2 Tim. 1:12). Ever since I can remember, I have heard people say, "I know *in* whom I have believed." That changes the meaning entirely. It suggests you can believe in Him and that will suffice. Paul knew Him. In Philippians, he was more explicit. "But what things were gain to me, those I counted loss for Christ. Yea doubtless, and I count all things but loss for the excellency of the knowledge of Christ Jesus my Lord" (Phil. 3:7-8). Paul continues in the next chapter: "That I may *know* him, and the power of his resurrection, and fellowship of his sufferings, being made conformable unto his death" (Phil. 4:10, emphasis mine).

The word "know," in the Greek is *ginōsko*. It is the basic word used to describe knowing a thing or person by experience. Paul uses the word often, especially when he talks about intimacy with the Lord. According to Bullinger, "It denotes a personal and true relation between the person knowing and the object known." It is the word used when describing the physical intimacy between a husband and wife. It hints at the mystical joining of spirits enjoyed only in the marriage bond.

The angel appeared to Mary saying, "Fear not, Mary: for thou hast found favor with God. And, behold, thou shalt conceive in thy womb, and bring forth a son, and shalt call his name Jesus" (Luke 1:30-31).

Mary, in disbelief, asked, "How shall this be, seeing I *know* not a man?" (Luke 1:34, emphasis mine).

Luke used the word *ginōsko* for the word "know." It portrays the most intimate human experience. Sadly, the sexual overtones in our society tend to obscure the beauty of the physical union in marriage. We must strive to preserve the original beauty of physical love as God originally intended. The intimate relationship between a man and wife mirrors the relationship Christ has with His Bride, the Church.

LIFE IS ABOUT RELATIONSHIPS

Solomon described the wonder of a man's relationship with a woman. "There are three things which are too wonderful for me, Four which I do not understand: The way of an eagle in the sky, the way of a serpent on a rock, the way of a ship in the middle of the sea, and the way of a man with a maid" (Prov. 30:18-19 NASB). When true, spiritual love exists between a husband and wife, their physical and emotional relationship becomes difficult to put into words. If we can get past the unsavory way relationships are portrayed by the media and cinema, we may recover the beautiful meaning God intended.

Jewish lore suggests the Song of Solomon may be the most important book in the Bible because it tells the story of human love. Life is about relationships. God's kingdom is about relationships. The Father, Son, and Holy Spirit existed in perfect, harmonious relationship before time began. Creation, I firmly believe, is God's desire to enjoy intimate fellowship with all created beings, especially man. God so loved us, He gave us His beloved Son to bring us back into relationship with Him. Adam and Eve had that relationship and lost it because they thought they knew better than God. Their disobedience separated them and all humanity from a loving Creator. Jesus became the door to divine intimacy between Creator and creature.

One question remains. How can a mortal person know God intimately? Start by believing you can. Dare to believe our Father desires to be precisely who He is—a Father who just happens to be God. Yes, He is our Creator. Yes, He is the Savior of the world. Yes, He is a righteous judge before whom every knee shall bow one day. Yet, more than anything, He is our Father.

WITHOUT SUFFERING WE CAN FORGET POWER

Dare to believe most things that have happened to you as a believer were used by God to bring you into intimacy with Him. On the other hand, I do not believe, as Augustine taught, that everything that happens is somehow God's will. As I mentioned earlier, I believe we are living in a spiritual warzone, and terrible things happen to innocent people during wartime.

Satan is the inspiration behind everything from war to weeds. Jesus said, "The kingdom of heaven is likened unto a man which sowed good seeds in his field: But while men slept, his enemy came and sowed tares among the wheat, and went his way" (Mt. 13:24-25). Tares are weeds resembling wheat. You can't pull them up without uprooting the wheat as well. According to Jesus, we should "Let both grow together until the harvest: and in the time of harvest I will say to the reapers, Gather ye together first the tares, and bind them in bundles to burn them: but gather the wheat into my barns" (Mt. 13:30). Satan is the enemy. If he can't start a war, he will plant weeds in the form of hypocrites. Judas became Jesus' tare and brought misery to Him and the disciples. Suffering seems to be part of life, even during times of peace.

We all want to know Him in the power of His resurrection, His supernatural life erupting inside us and spilling out into the lives of others. Lest we forget, Paul, inspired by the Holy Spirit, ends his revelation in Philippians 3:10 with our need to know Christ in the "fellowship of His sufferings." If only he had left off a moment earlier and not included suffering. Alas, without suffering, we can forget power. Knowing Him in His power requires knowing Him in His suffering. Intimacy and suffering are married and are the foundation of power.

It is no accident Paul refers to the fellowship of His suffering. The original word for "fellowship" is *koinonía*. Strong defines fellowship as "sharing, partnering and having social intercourse with." It speaks of close experiential knowledge. Suffering is not something we endure so much as it is something we need. Suffering is the fertilizer of true spiritual growth.

Peter adds beautiful insight when he reminds us, "Beloved, think it not strange concerning the fiery trial which is to try you" (1 Pet. 4:12-13). The word "strange" is from the Greek word *xénos,* which, according to Strong, means "foreign or alien." Marshall captures the meaning when he translates, "Beloved, be not surprised [at] the fiery trial happening among [in] you."

Trials should not surprise us, but they always seem to, don't they? Instead of catching us by surprise, trials should become a normal and necessary ingredient to spiritual balance and maturity. Don't view suffering as strange or even unusual. Embrace suffering as par for the Christian course and a prerequisite to God's power.

I'M STILL WORKING ON REJOICING IN THE MIDST OF THE FIRE

When fiery trials come our way, we should embrace them—not as surprises, but as opportunities to rejoice. I, for one, have great difficulty rejoicing when things seem to be breaking loose around me. At the same time, when I look back at every fiery trial I ever experienced, I can rejoice when I remember the wonderful things the Lord did to insure my survival. Yet, in spite of His proven faithfulness in the past, I'm still working on rejoicing in the midst of the fire. I know fire refines and purifies, but it is also very painful. In fact, under certain circumstances, fire can be deadly, especially when it comes to our pride.

When we realize the essential connection between suffering and intimacy, we gain the freedom to grow in grace and power. Peter sums up his epistles with these words: "But grow *in* grace and *in* the knowledge of our Lord and Savior Jesus Christ" (2 Pet. 3:18, emphasis mine). Notice, we don't grow *into* grace and we don't grow *into* knowledge. We grow in knowledge and intimacy as we learn to trust Him fully.

This is the same Peter who told us in his first epistle to see suffering, not as a strange or surprising thing, but as a necessary part of our experience as followers of Jesus. The benefit of suffering is knowing Him intimately and we grow in that intimacy little by little every day. Suffering breeds intimacy. Suffering builds character. Suffering infuses empathy. Suffering smothers pride. Ultimately, suffering releases resurrection life. We should not look for suffering, nor should we resist it as something strange. Even if we suffer because of wrong decisions, God will use it for our good. In that case, "all things work together for good" (Rom. 8:28).

FAITH COMES FROM HEARING GOD'S VOICE

Jesus learned obedience by the things He suffered, according to Hebrews 5:8. Another of my favorite verses is, "Faith cometh by hearing, and hearing by the word of God" (Rom. 10:17). As I mentioned in an earlier chapter, the phrase "the word of God," in the original language, is actually "a *rhema* of Christ." *Rhema* suggests not merely what the Bible says, but what Christ Himself is saying today. Jesus made that clear when He said, "My sheep hear my voice, and I know them, and they follow me" (John 10:27).

Faith, we can conclude, comes from hearing God's voice. The better we know Him, the more intimate we become with Him. The more intimate we grow, the easier it is to hear His voice.

Obedience is a curious thing. It presupposes something important. We tend to over-spiritualize Biblical principles. I have heard some pretty involved teaching about obeying God. The underlying reality of obedience is simple indeed. To obey Him, you must be able to *hear* Him. Is it possible to hear the voice of the Lord Jesus Christ today? If Jesus said, "My sheep hear my voice," that's good enough for me. God is not dead; He's just particular about who He talks to nowadays. He is, however, always looking for people who will listen. I believe He can speak for Himself. I believe He wants us to hear.

When Jesus and Peter reached the boat after miraculously walking on water, the disciples made a timeless acknowledgment. "And when they were come into the ship, the wind ceased. Then they that were in the ship came and worshipped him, saying, Of a truth thou art the Son of God" (Mt. 14:32-33). They finally knew who He was. That experience soon led each disciple to know Jesus more intimately. That should be great consolation to those of us who strive to know Him today.

We are not required to have walked with Him on earth. We need only acknowledge with the disciples, "Of a truth thou art the Son of God." He will take care of the rest. The Holy Spirit will gently draw each of us into intimacy with Himself, the Lord Jesus and our loving Father.

Paul's heartfelt desire—"That I may know Him"—was all the Holy Spirit needed to mold the apostle into the image of Christ. Paul became the instrument that helped the early church make an impact for Christ on earth that endures to this day.

We have the same Holy Spirit. He sees in each of us a future apostle, prophet, evangelist, pastor, or teacher. We can make our own imprint on earth for the Lord of Glory. All He needs is our belief that we can know Him intimately. Stop looking for more faith. Start believing you can know the Lord and know Him well. Faith is an organic outgrowth of intimacy with the Lord.

THERE IS NO SECRET FORMULA

I'm sorry if you read this book hoping for some secret formula to maximize your faith and see fabulous answers to prayer. There is no secret formula. I looked for one for decades. The fact that I searched for such a shortcut only served to expose my selfishness. I wanted miracle faith for my own enjoyment. I missed the point of true Christian living. I knew I should deny myself, but had no idea how or why.

Slowly, over the years, key verses began to make an impact, especially after I began to read the Bible just to see what it said. I learned early in my Christian experience that my selfishness had to go. Consequently, I spent years wondering when self would subside and the Holy Spirit would begin to dominate my heart. The Old Testament provides the answer.

God told the Israelites how He would deal with their enemies before they entered Canaan. He said, "I will not drive them out before you in a single year, that the land may not become desolate and the beasts of the field become too numerous for you. I will drive them out before you *little by little*, until you become fruitful and take possession of the land" (Ex. 23:29-30 NASB, emphasis mine). Our greatest enemy is self and the Lord deals with self one step at a time. If we knew the challenge He faced to move us from self-centered, to God-centered living, we may not have lasted the course. Thankfully, like the Children of Israel, He deals with self little by little.

The Holy Spirit transforms us slowly but surely into the image of Christ until, as Paul explains, "We all, with unveiled face beholding as in a mirror the glory of the Lord, are being transformed into the same image from glory to glory" (2 Cor. 3:18 NASB). The word "transformed" is from the Greek word *metamorphóo*. That word, as you might have guessed, is the root word for "metamorphosis," defined by Webster as "a change of physical form, structure or substance especially by supernatural means." I immediately think of the breathtaking transformation butterflies experience.

An adult butterfly lays its eggs. Caterpillars hatch from the eggs and attach themselves to a tree branch. Hanging upside down, the caterpillar sheds its old skin and dons a new coat. During this cocoon (or pupa) stage, the internal systems develop, along with external adult structures such as wings and legs. Eventually, the cocoon breaks open and an adult butterfly emerges with wet, crumpled wings. The wings slowly dry, take shape, and, majestically, the butterfly floats away, full of life and regal beauty.

The maximum lifespan of the average butterfly, including development, is six months. Some desert species are the exception and spend up to seven years in the development stage. All only spend twenty to forty days as an adult. The majority of a butterfly's life is spent in growth and development. Flying time is relatively short compared to the growth process.

I am convinced the Christian life is similar. Too often, a believer wants to fly before growth and development are complete. Without the proper time in the developmental stages, the adult butterfly's wings will be stunted and imperfect. Flight, if possible at all, will be irregular and sporadic.

James said, "Let not many of you become teachers, my brethren, knowing that as such we shall incur [receive] a stricter judgment" (James 3:1 NASB). He implored each of us to avoid rushing to become a spiritual leader.

Teaching is the first rung on the five-fold ministry ladder, ascending to pastor, evangelist, prophet, and apostle. We need patience, patience, patience. Get to know the Lord intimately before you try to fly. Knowing His word is not the same as knowing Him. Satan knows the Word, but he will never know the Lord the way we do. The Word of God teaches us clearly that we can know Him as intimately as a mother knows her newborn baby.

God asks the question, "Can a woman forget her nursing child, And have no compassion on the son of her womb? Even these may forget, but I will not forget you. Behold, I have inscribed you on the palms of My hands" (Is. 49:15-16 NASB). A nursing mother may forget her newborn, but God will never forget you. Your name is tattooed on the palm of His hand.

I leave you with a simple lesson from life. I love my wife. We dated, put on our best faces for each other, and for a time courted long distance via the post office and Ma Bell.

My wife kept all those love letters we wrote to each other. I confess, I haven't looked at them for some time. We could read and enjoy them but, given the choice, we would rather just hold each other. We should always enjoy God's word, His love letter to us, but I would rather be with Him and talk with Him than just read about Him. Thankfully, He gave us the privilege to do both. Love His word—*love Him more*.

May we each enjoy the stunning reality Thomas experienced when he first saw Jesus after His resurrection. John tells the story beautifully.

> But Thomas, one of the twelve, called Didymus, was not with them when Jesus came.
>
> So the other disciples therefore were saying to him, "We have seen the Lord!" But he said to them, "Unless I shall see in his hands the imprint of the nails,

and put my finger into the place of the nails, and put my hand into His side, I will not believe."

After eight days again His disciples were inside, and Thomas with them. Jesus came, the doors having been shut, and stood in their midst, and said, "Peace be with you."

Then He said to Thomas, "Reach here your finger and see My hands; and reach here your hand and put it into My side; and be not unbelieving, but believing."

Thomas answered and said to him, "My Lord and my God!"

Jesus said to him, "Thomas, because you have seen me, have you believed? Blessed are they who did not see, and yet believed."

(John 20:24-29 NASB)

Thomas finally knew, without question, that Christ was fully alive. At that moment, his intimacy with Christ began to flourish. We have not seen Him as Thomas did, but we can still know Him just as intimately. We are the "Blessed" ones Jesus talked about. We have never seen Him, yet we believe just as surely as Thomas believed.

I hope I have influenced you to see the Scriptural connection between intimacy and faith. Thomas became intimate with Christ after His resurrection. So can we. We may not get to touch the nail prints in His hands, but we can certainly get to know Him and know Him well. John gave a beautiful summary when he said, "Many other signs [attesting miracles] therefore Jesus also performed in the presence of the disciples, which are not written in this book; but these have been written, that you may believe that Jesus is the Christ the Son of God; and that believing you may have life in His name" (John 20:30-31 NASB).

Remember, the life we are talking about is resurrection life. We refer to it as eternal life.

What is eternal life? Is it living forever? Perhaps not. Everyone will live forever in one place or another. Jesus gave us a simple definition of eternal life and I missed it for years. It is Jesus' definition. Are you ready?

"This is eternal life, that they may *know* Thee, the only true God, and Jesus Christ, whom Thou hast sent" (John 17:3 NASB, emphasis mine). Can it be that simple?

Believing is faith acted out. It is faith with feet, if you please. Faith in action generates eternal life, and that life is defined as knowing the Lord of Glory intimately and personally. Relax and let Him lead you into intimacy. Little by little, you will find yourself joining Him in His earthly ministry. Look forward to the moment when you finally let go the main mast and step out to meet the Master on the water.

Chapter 14

WON'T THEY COME IF WE HAVE MIRACLES?

Join any discussion in a typical Sunday school class and the conversation will often center around the probability that we don't pray enough and that is why we don't see miracles today. If we pray and fast more, we tell ourselves, we will have miracles in our midst and the world will flock to our doors. Yet no one can tell us just how much extra prayer and fasting is enough to do the trick. If we knew the answer to that question, we would all exert the proper amount and, presto, we would enjoy New Testament miracles and standing room only in our churches.

Discussions on faith often seem to degenerate to reasoning that a lack of miracles points to our lack faith. We wrongfully assume faith will automatically lead to miracles and we further assume miracles are the reason God gives us faith. Our major challenge is understanding the need for balance.

Which came first, the chicken or the egg? Which came first, faith or miracles? Miracles may encourage faith, but miracles will never produce faith. God alone produces faith and He alone metes out sufficient faith to each believer. Miracles can attract unbelievers, and some may trust Christ as a result. The drama and awe of miracles, however, have never produced staying power in new converts. Faith, and faith alone, keeps us in step with the Man from Galilee.

JESUS' RESULTS WERE DISMAL

Let us first look at Jesus' life of faith and miracles. During three years of a miraculous ministry like the world had never seen, He had large crowds, avid followers, and fame and notoriety that permeated an entire nation and beyond. Yet, despite all that, Jesus' results were dismal. Under pressure, his disciples left Him and refused to be identified with Him. The same masses who watched Him work miracles, from healing the blind to raising the dead, joined the throng who cried out for His blood. To their credit, I am sure many who received miracles at His touch were silent on that dark day and found it impossible to join the chant, "Crucify him, away with Him!" At the same time, those who believed in the Nazarene did not dare publicly defend Him in the hour of His death for fear of their own safety.

I have believed for decades that miracles are part of every believer's right in Christ. I have also taught that miracles may attract the curious, the skeptical, and the unrighteous, but miracles will not produce dedicated believers or keep them secure in the faith. The fact remains, after His miraculous ministry, His undeniable resurrection, and His appearance to the disciples after He rose from dead, His following was sparse. His earthly ministry did not qualify as a success.

Where were the five thousand He miraculously fed with five loaves of bread and two fish? Where were the multitudes that saw His miracles? Where were the tens of thousands who followed Him ardently during His powerful, but brief, ministry? Let's be realistic. When the dust settled, only one hundred and twenty waited in the upper room for the promised Holy Spirit. Just who they were, we cannot say.

Included among the faithful were the eleven disciples who eventually led the early church to "turn the world upside down" (Acts 17:6). Just over one hundred remained of all the thousands who heard Him teach and watched Him work incredible miracles day after day for three years. Several hundred probably crowded into that upper room initially to "wait for the promise of the Father" (Acts 1:4). As hours turned into days, I imagine one follower after another slipped quietly out the door, their faith surrendering to doubt and impatience.

Like Gideon's three hundred, the hundred and twenty refused to give up or give in to unbelief. God chose Gideon to lead a troop to deliver Israel from the Midianites who threatened invasion. God told Gideon the existing army was too large to send against the Midianites. He was sure the Israelites would take credit for the victory, saying, "Mine own hand hath saved me" (Judges 7:2). Therefore, He told Gideon to whittle the numbers down by offering a way out, saying, "Whosoever is fearful and afraid, let him return and depart early from mount Gilead" (v. 3). Twenty-two thousand went home. Ten thousand remained.

Then, God told Gideon to invite the men to drink from a nearby water source, explaining, those who drink "putting their hand to their mouth," (v. 6) will be the ones chosen to fight. Only three hundred drank the prescribed way. Each of the others, kneeling and drinking with their faces in the water, drank "of the water with his tongue, as a dog lappeth" (v. 5).

Commentators suggest the soldiers who used their hands to drink, did so to keep their eyes on the battlefield. Those kneeling and drinking saw only their own reflections and that made them vulnerable to attack. Just why God chose only three hundred is anyone's guess. A meager few hundred men routed an enemy army of thousands because God was in it. In a day when numbers mean success in business and ministry, perhaps we should revisit God's word to relearn His ways. He doesn't need a multitude with ability; He needs only a few who are simply available. He doesn't ask about a person's talents, education, or background. God calls those who are willing to trust Him without trying to impress Him.

Deny yourself and volunteer to be one of God's select few. You won't get any credit for what happens, but you may be amazed at what He does through you.

GOD DID THE IMPOSSIBLE WITH A HANDFUL

A mere hundred and twenty obeyed Jesus and waited in the upper room. Their patience and faith paid off when God filled them with the power of His Holy Spirit on the Day of Pentecost. The world has never been the same. As usual, God did the impossible with a handful.

Another Gospel story helps us understand the futility of miracles to draw and keep the lost. It involves a beggar called Lazarus and a nameless rich man (Luke 16:19-31). According to Jesus, they both died. Lazarus the beggar "was carried by the angels into Abraham's bosom" (v. 22). The rich man, on the other hand, found himself in a different realm. "In hell he lift up his eyes, being in torments, and seeth Abraham afar off, and Lazarus in his bosom" (v. 23). From his place of torment, the rich man "cried and said, Father Abraham, have mercy on me, and send Lazarus that he may dip the tip of his finger in water, and cool my tongue; for I am tormented in this flame" (v. 24). Abraham refused.

Forgetting himself for a moment, the rich man thought of his surviving brothers and made a strange request. "I pray thee therefore, father, that thou wouldest send him to my father's house: For I have five brethren; that he may testify unto them, lest they also come into this place of torment" (vs. 27-28).

Abraham replied, "They have Moses and the prophets; let them hear them" (v. 29). Abraham insisted that the truth found in the Old Testament is enough to convince his brothers to walk righteously before God and avoid hell's torments.

The rich man, refusing to hear the truth, said, "Nay, father Abraham: but if one went unto them from the dead, they will repent."

"And he said unto him, If they hear not Moses and the prophets, *neither will they be persuaded, though one rose from the dead*" (Luke 16:30-31, emphasis mine).

TRUE FAITH NEVER REQUIRES VISIBLE EVIDENCE

There you have it. Jesus Himself laid down the guiding principle. Even the miracle of a resurrection is not enough to change a man's mind. Miracles have never been the primary tool of persuasion to bring the lost to repentance. Faith in God Himself is the only way to peace and true security. The truth of the Gospel, accompanied by the gentle tugging of the Holy Spirit, draws people to Christ.

Thomas doubted the fact of Christ's resurrection until he saw the scars in His hands and believed. Jesus' words still echo the miracle of God-given faith. "Thomas, because thou hast seen me, thou hast believed: blessed are they that have not seen and yet have believed" (John 20:29). True faith never requires visible evidence. "For we walk by faith, not by sight" (2 Cor. 5:7). When John the Baptist first saw Jesus, he declared, "Behold the Lamb of God" (John 1:29). He could have said, "Look who's here!"

Believers today often say, "I wish I could have lived when Jesus did." I have good news—You do! Look who's here!

Chapter 15

WE LIVE FOR HIM

There is an unwritten rule among schoolteachers that suggests ninth graders need to hear something seven times before it sinks in. That is easy to verify. When handing out daily class work to students, the teacher will repeatedly tell students not to write on the worksheet, but use their own paper. Invariably, within minutes, one of the students will ask, "Can we write on this?"

The next time you order hamburgers and fries and say "That's to go," the clerk will almost always ask, "Is that for here or to go?" There seems to be a disease in this culture that induces people to listen without hearing.

That must have been a problem in Jesus' day as well. Three times in the second chapter of the book of Revelation, and three more times in chapter three, Jesus said, "He who has an ear, let him hear what the Spirit says to the churches" (Rev. 2:7, 17, 29; 3:6, 13, 22 NASB). Spiritual deafness was certainly a problem in Isaiah's day. The prophet accused Israel, saying, "For the heart of this people is waxed gross, and their ears are dull of hearing" (Acts 28:27).

This dullness of hearing takes a sinister twist in our day, especially among church folk. Timothy says, "For the time will come when they will not endure sound doctrine; but after their own lusts shall they heap to themselves teachers, having itching ears; And they shall turn away their ears from the truth, and shall be turned unto fables" (2 Tim. 4:3-4). The fables are more a philosophy than a series of mythical tales. The modern, "What about me?" mindset demands that we look out for number one. When we focus on ourselves, we tend to show little interest in what others are saying unless it pertains to us.

Today a malignant spirit of self-love and self-sufficiency competes against the love of God for the hearts of men. Psychologists preach self-esteem as the one thing everyone needs to succeed in life. Consequently, modern man is full of himself. Ask anyone a question about himself and get ready for a lengthy response. Self-love will fuel the one-way conversation until you find yourself making excuses to leave.

That brings me to the point of this chapter. Most of our teaching, most of our preaching, and most of our worship music is far more man-centered than God-centered. Too often, we leave a church service thinking entirely about ourselves and little about the Lord. Man-centered preaching makes us focus on our need to stop doing this and start doing that, whatever this and that turns out to be that day. God-centered preaching makes us think about the Lord of Glory. I'd rather think about Him and His goodness than me and my shortcomings.

MAN-CENTERED THINKING IS SUFFOCATING BELIEVERS TODAY

Daniel predicted that end-time demonic forces would "speak great words against the most High, and shall wear out the saints of the most High" (Dan. 7:25). Satan's goal is to wear us out—or, more accurately, to wear us down. Man-centered thinking is suffocating believers today. The anti-Christian values dominant in this world clutter our minds with subtle messages of materialism and the importance of self-esteem as if mere wealth and a higher self-image would solve all our problems. The modern focus on self-improvement just makes self more entrenched than ever. Self doesn't need a better image—it needs the cross.

The true remnant today realizes the utter importance of the centrality of Christ. Satan trembles at the thought that the Church might wake up and make Christ preeminent. He seems to sense the world is about to see what can happen when God's children put Him first in all things.

On the other hand, those with itching ears want what they want, when they want it, and get frustrated when the answer to their prayer lingers. They aren't faithless; they are just selfish. Faith wanes when self takes precedence over Christ. Paul reminds us, "And he [Christ] is before all things, and by him all things consist. And he is the head of the body, the church: who is the beginning, the firstborn from the dead; *that in all things he might have the preeminence*" (Col. 1:17-18, emphasis mine). He must be more important to you and me than our comfort, our security, and our personal desires.

I heard Billy Graham say years ago, "He's either Lord of all, or He's not Lord at all." Too many believers today call Him Lord just to secure His blessing on their plans. It doesn't work that way. When we dare call Him *Lord,* we give Him the right to tell us what to do and we give up our right to say, "No."

True believers, delivered from their selfish desires, understand the testimony of the twenty-four elders recorded in the book of Revelation. "The four and twenty elders fall down before him that sat on the throne, and worship him that liveth for ever and ever, and cast their crowns before the throne, saying, Thou art worthy, O Lord, to receive glory and honor and power; for that hast created all things, and for thy pleasure they are and were created" (Rev. 4:10-11).

It really is about Him. We are blessed to be included in the plan of God, but Christ is always God's focus. Because we are in Christ, we become recipients of God's blessing. We deserve nothing on our own merits.

Faith tenaciously declares, *It's not I—it's Christ.* He must become the preeminent One in our lives. We should remember the ageless question, "Why am I here?"—or, as David put it, "What is man, that thou art mindful of him?" (Ps. 8:4). Why did God create man? Our Creator answers: "I have created him for my glory, I have formed him; yea, I have made him" (Is. 43:7). God in Christ, through the power of the Holy Spirit, created all things for His pleasure and enjoyment. Ultimately, He made man for Himself.

The fabulous thing about His motivation to create is the fact that it gives our Father great pleasure to love us and bless us beyond our wildest dreams.

If you can consciously strive to stop living for yourself and start living for Him, the Holy Spirit will, inch by spiritual inch, move you from self-centered thinking to a Christ-centered mindset. It won't be a new level or even a breakthrough; it will be a natural transition into the selfless living the cross of Christ demands. Miracle-working faith will become an organic by-product of your new and improved "not I, but Christ" attitude. Only then will you begin to realize you have enough faith and find the courage to stop asking for more.

There are many anti-Christian voices clamoring for our attention today. I will conclude this discussion on faith by briefly addressing one of the most damnable theories ever to find its way into church ideology. Secular psychologists in the 1940s insisted that we must learn to love ourselves before we can properly love others. Perhaps, hoping the church world would take notice, they used the words of Jesus, "Thou shalt love thy neighbor as thyself" (Mt. 19:19). Sad to say, the church not only took notice, she swallowed it hook, line, and sinker. By the mid-1970s, self-love had become part of our unofficial declaration of faith. We have been busy trying to love ourselves ever since along with building up our self-esteem and our self-image. Self-love is still a popular subject to this day.

Back in the mid-1980s, on a Friday after work, I made a hurried seventy-mile drive to a conference at our local church campground. As anticipated, I was late for the seven o'clock meeting and arrived just after the keynote speaker began his address. As I found one of the few seats left, the teacher pointed to his chart and explained our need to understand the three important ways to love.

He said, "First and foremost, we must love God. Secondly, we must learn to love ourselves, so, finally, we can properly love our neighbors."

I remember saying to myself, "Jesus said we should love God and love our neighbor, but I don't remember Him saying we should love ourselves." I let it go and enjoyed the rest of the conference. I didn't think about it again until my good friend, Herb, told me about a book he had recently read on the subject of self-love.

SELF-LOVE BECAME A HOUSEHOLD TERM VIRTUALLY OVERNIGHT

Herb insisted, "Ted, you have to read *The Danger of Self-Love* by Paul Brownback." To quote Mr. Brownback in chapter one, "Self-love became a household term virtually overnight. It was a vivid occurrence of love at first sight. This concept and Christian thinking skipped the engagement period and were joined in a very sudden marriage."

I would suggest further, it was a welcome idea for Christians with "itching ears" (2 Tim. 4:3-4). It made so much sense to a generation of believers looking for some new secret to Christian living. It implied that Christ's command to love our neighbor is somehow a command to love ourselves first. Self climbed down from the cross and became the center of attention in Christian growth forums.

To make matters worse, the Christian market has been flooded with books on the subject of self-love since the mid-70s. Many fail to realize that loving yourself and denying yourself are at eternal odds with each other.

As revival fires cool in every generation that experiences renewal, the presence of Christ Himself slowly but surely fades. Then we become gullible to any new thing that stirs excitement in the church world. The early Church turned the world upside down because the living Christ was so real and present in their midst. They didn't worry about loving themselves or building up their own self-image. That didn't even occur to early believers. They unselfishly followed the Christ, who said, "Whosoever will come after me, let him deny himself, and take up his cross, and follow me" (Mark 8:34). They embraced the cross, denied themselves, focused on Christ, and turned the world upside down.

If you are busy denying yourself, you won't have the time or energy to love yourself. By the way, what do you see in yourself that is really worth loving? Take a lesson from Christ Himself. A rich young ruler approached Him and said, "Good Master, what good thing shall I do, that I may have eternal life?"

Jesus answered, "Why callest thou me good? there is none good but one, that is, God" (Mt. 19:16-17). Because He was fully man, even Christ saw nothing good in Himself. Add to that Paul's claim, "For I know that nothing good dwells in me, that is, in my flesh" (Rom. 7:18 NASB).

Some of you may still be shocked at my assertion that loving ourselves is a doctrine found nowhere in Scripture. The thing that still astounds me about this unholy teaching is the fact that few, other than Dr. Brownback, have bothered to investigate Scripture to see if self-love was sound teaching. A casual reading of the New Testament and its references to love would have stopped this heinous self-love dogma dead in its Satanic tracks. Remember, Satan wants us to focus on ourselves instead of Christ. His subtle introduction of the self-love philosophy worked perfectly.

Here are some verses for thought. Paul wastes no time worrying about offending the self-love gurus when he says, "This know also, that in the last days perilous times shall come. For men shall be *lovers of their own selves*. . . ." He goes on to describe those who love themselves as "covetous, boasters, proud, blasphemers, disobedient to parents, unthankful, unholy. . . ." The list goes on until Paul concludes saying men will be "lovers of pleasures more than lovers of God" (2 Tim. 3:1–4, emphasis mine).

"Wait," you protest. "We're not like that!"

I agree. If you are truly living for Christ, you won't be guilty of those sins. Why, then, would you want to be identified with the folks who not only love themselves, but love pleasure more than they love God? On a lighter note, Ben Franklin said, "He that falls in love with himself will have no rivals."

Self-love encourages us to tell ourselves how deserving we are of good things, along with how good we are. Self-love advocates tell us to verbalize our wonderfulness by saying things like, "I'm wonderful, I'm beautiful, I love myself because I am loveable and I deserve to be loved." I need to change the subject before my gag mechanism kicks in.

Are you still not convinced? Paul said, "For no one ever hated his own flesh, but nourishes and cherishes it, just as Christ also does [nourish and cherish] the church" (Ephesians 5:29 NASB). Do you see it? We love our flesh as much as Christ loves the church. Do we really need to learn to love ourselves before we can properly love others? Not according to this verse: "But as touching brotherly love ye need not that I write unto you: for ye yourselves are taught of God to love one another" (1 Thess. 4:9). God Himself teaches us to love one another. He doesn't need our help and He certainly doesn't need our self-love as a teaching tool.

He who denied Himself and gave Himself for us still admonishes us to deny ourselves, take up His cross, and follow Him. Focus on yourself and faith will be confusing and elusive. Purpose in your heart to focus more on Christ and less on self. That is a simple exercise of the mind. "You are what you eat," nutritionists tell us. Solomon tells us we are what we think. "As he thinketh in his heart, so is he" (Proverbs 23:7). Stop thinking about yourself. It has no spiritual benefit.

Your faith will take root and mature in direct proportion to your ever-increasing focus on the Master. Fix your mind on Christ and watch your alleged need for more faith dissipate. You have all the faith you will ever need.

ADDENDUM

"Howbeit this kind goeth not out but by prayer and fasting" (Matthew 17:21).

As a young Christian, I heard teaching that suggested only those who fast and pray can cast out demons, which meant something beyond faith was required. It puzzled me for years. Studying ancient manuscripts solved the puzzle.

Several New Testament verses have words in italics. Romans 8:31 is an example: "What shall we say to these things? If god *be* for us, who *can be* against us?" Adding *be* and *can be* make the verse easier to read. Those words are not in the oldest manuscripts, but Bible scholars accept the additional wording because literal translations from Greek to English are difficult to follow.

A few other verses have added words that are not in the oldest manuscripts. That means they were added later (perhaps by translators who were unconsciously influenced by their personal theological views). These additions are designated as *spurious* because they change the meaning of a verse or add meaning that is unjustified. *Spurious* means "not genuine."

Matthew 17:21 is an example, as is Mark 9:29. In both verses, the words "and fasting" are missing from the two oldest manuscripts, the Codex Sinaiticus and the Vatican #1209, both dating from the early fourth century.

Over time, small insights appeared in Bible translations that were not in older manuscripts. Most Bibles explain these spurious additions in the margin and point to their omission in older manuscripts. Several newer translations omit spurious verses altogether such as the Revised Standard Version published in 1952 and the more recent and popular New International Version, published in 1978. The New American Standard Bible encloses Matthew 17:21 in brackets and notes in the margin, "Many manuscripts do not contain this verse."

Omitting spurious words does not detract from the purity of the text in question and makes the verses clearer and truer to the context of the passage.

BIBLIOGRAPHY

Boyd, Gregory. 2001. *Satan and the Problem of Evil.* Downers Grove: InterVarsity Press. Reference used by permission.

Brownback, Paul. 1982. *The Danger of Self-love.* Chicago: Moody Press. Quote used by permission.

Bullinger, Ethelbert. 1957. *A Critical Lexicon and Concordance.* London: The Lamp Press Ltd.

Gesenius, William. 1979. *Gesenius' Hebrew and Chaldee Lexicon.* Grand Rapids: Baker Book House.

Marshall, Alfred. 1958. *The Interlinear Greek-English New Testament.* Grand Rapids: Zondervan Publishing House.

Strong, James. 1990. *New Strong's exhaustive concordance of the Bible.* Nashville: Thomas Nelson Publishers.

Unger, Merrill. 1957. *Unger's Bible Dictionary.* Chicago: Moody Press. Jericho references used by permission.

Merriam-Webster. 1997. *The Merriam-Webster Dictionary.* Springfield, MA: Merriam-Webster, Inc.

ABOUT THE AUTHOR

Ted Bowman has served as pastor, associate pastor, evangelist, Christian school principal, seminar teacher, and conference speaker, as well as a public school teacher.

His book on faith is the result of nearly half a century of living for Christ. Balking at the tendency of Christian leaders to give complicated answers to simple questions, Ted writes about the simplicity of the faith God gives to each believer. Simply put, he insists God gives to each of us a measure of faith that will prove to be enough. More faith is not necessary.

In 2007, his wife, Judith, published her first book, *THE FIERY FURNACE OF CANCER: A Survival Guide for Families Coping With Cancer.* That first effort was Judith's passion, the result of a year of chemotherapy with their daughter Sarah. Not finding a simple book telling her what to expect during standard cancer treatment, Judith wrote one. It answers the question, "Cancer has touched my family; now what?"

Based on a year of detailed journal notes, she describes everything from the onset of the diagnosis, to chemotherapy side effects, doctors' attitudes, nurses' empathy, hospital conditions, and everything she and her family experienced that stressful year.

Telling her story in friendly yet candid terms, Judith hopes to spare others the potentially overwhelming anxiety that accompanies the doctor's news, "It's cancer."

Judith's husband, Ted, says it well: "We were overwhelmed. No one else need be."

To order books, go to *http://www.jcpublishers.net*

or call 863-875-6071.

Also available from any online bookseller.

You can email *ted@jcpublishers.net*

or

judith@jcpublishers.com.

Mailing address:

Ted and Judith Bowman
4844 Osprey Way
Winter Haven, FL 33881

www.ingramcontent.com/pod-product-compliance
Lightning Source LLC
LaVergne TN
LVHW051123080426
835510LV00018B/2204